SLOW COOKER DESSERTS

SLOW COOKER
DESSERTS

Oh So Easy, Oh So Delicious!

ROXANNE WYSS

AND

KATHY MOORE

PHOTOGRAPHS BY JENNIFER DAVICK

ST. MARTIN'S GRIFFIN
NEW YORK

www.stmartins.com

Designed by Jennifer Daddio / Bookmark Design & Media Inc.

The Library of Congress Cataloging-in-Publication Data is available upon request.

ISBN 978-1-250-05967-3 (paper over board)
ISBN 978-1-4668-6505-1 (e-book)

St. Martin's Griffin books may be purchased for educational, business, or promotional use. For information on bulk purchases, please contact the Macmillan Corporate and Premium Sales Department at 1-800-221-7945, extension 5442, or write to specialmarkets@macmillan.com.

First Edition: September 2015

10 9 8 7 6 5 4 3 2 1

We dedicate this book to
our friendship,
for friendship is such a sweet part of life.

Our cherished friendship began in a test kitchen more than thirty years ago.
We have been business colleagues and friends ever since,
and what a blessing that has been!

CONTENTS

FRUITS

FONDUES AND CONFECTIONS

INTRODUCTION

Who doesn't love dessert? Some of us crave a piece of decadent cheesecake or a big slice of chocolate cake, while others cannot resist a bowl of warm, sweet fruit cobbler. The captivating aroma of cinnamon and those drips and drizzles of chocolate and caramel are tempting, and you know you just have to have a bite, a spoonful, or a bowl of satisfying goodness.

Slow Cooker Desserts captures the best of desserts—those special treats that transform meals into extraordinary celebrations—and bakes them to perfection, slowly, in a slow cooker.

In a slow cooker? Yes, in that familiar slow cooker!

Almost everyone owns a slow cooker, and today, many people own more than one. Most folks wouldn't think of making a pot of chili, soup, or stew on a cold winter day without one. You cannot attend a party without dipping a chip into a slow cooker full of spicy Mexican cheese dip. The flavor of the food cooked in the slow cooker is wonderful, and for all of the busy cooks in the world (and that includes us), the slow cooker offers unsurpassed convenience and ease.

Now, we have captured the scrumptious flavors and easy preparation and sweetened the deal. The results are the best desserts you can imagine. Bake a fantastic cake, cheesecake, bread pudding, cobbler, or crisp in your slow cooker. You can simmer the finest fruit dessert, heat the most luscious fondue, or effortlessly melt the chocolate for decadent candies, all using that favorite slow cooker you already own. The best part is that all of these desserts are prepared in the slow cooker, not because that preparation method would be a plausible option, but instead, because the slow, even heat and moist environment makes the ideal cooking method and gives you the best flavor.

SLOW COOKER BRANDS AND TYPES

The recipes in this book were tested in a slow cooker with a stoneware bowl or vessel set in a heating base. In this design, the heat wraps around the sides of the stoneware. The recipes were not tested in "multi-pots" or appliances that are designed to cook at various settings, such as simmer, stew, and deep-fry, as well as slow cooking.

The particular brand does not matter, so you can use that Crock-Pot slow cooker—or any other brand you might have. We understand that many people call the slow cooker by that common trade name. In fact, we started our career in the test kitchen of Rival Manufacturing Company—the company that started the slow cooker craze by introducing the Crock-Pot slow cooker. Today, there are many brands of slow cookers to choose from, and you can use the brand you prefer.

WHAT SIZE AND SHAPE OF SLOW COOKER?

In *Slow Cooker Desserts,* you will find a recipe for any size and shape of slow cooker you might own.

Large Slow Cookers	5 quarts or larger, round or oval	Cakes, cheesecakes, cobblers, crisps
Medium Slow Cookers	3½ to 5 quarts, round or oval	Cobblers, crisps, puddings
Small Slow Cookers	1 to 2 quarts, round	Fondues

Each recipe gives a suggested size of slow cooker to use. If you wish to use another size of slow cooker, you can do so. However, do not overfill the slow cooker, and be sure the lid rests flat on the slow cooker. If you use a larger slow cooker than specified in the recipe, leaving the slow cooker less than half full, you may need to reduce the cooking time, and you should definitely check the dessert as it cooks to avoid burning or overcooking.

COOKING IN THE SLOW COOKER

Spray the slow cooker with nonstick spray to make cleanup easier. When baking in a springform pan, there is no need to spray the slow cooker first with nonstick spray. Put the ingredients in the slow cooker and put the lid on the vessel.

The recipes list which heat setting to use, low or high, to cook or bake the dessert. Cook for the time and at the heat setting recommended in the recipe. Check the baking progress at the minimum cooking time listed. The recipes give tips so you can check to be sure they are done; if the dessert is not quite done, place the lid back on the slow cooker, continue cooking on the listed heat setting, and test again in 15 to 30 minutes.

One convenient aspect of slow cooking, even when slow cooking a dessert, is that you are free to do other tasks or run errands while the slow cooker does its magic. Another bonus is that timing is not as exact as when baking in an oven—baking in the oven for an extra minute or two may cause overbrowning, but not so with the slow cooker. Follow the recommended times, but if the phone or doorbell rings while the slow cooker is running, an extra 5 or 10 minutes will not ruin your efforts.

Slow cookers do not have a thermostat—so the actual temperature will vary with the brand, size, and shape of the cooker, the electrical voltage, and even the stoneware. After a use or two, you will be more familiar with your slow cooker and will know if the treats you bake in your slow cooker are usually done at the minimum or maximum time listed.

We have observed a change in slow cookers over the years—originally, they were very slow. Even on the high setting, the appliance cooked very slowly. If you are lucky enough to have a slow cooker that is ten to fifteen years old or older, you can slow cook the most delicious chicken or stew you could imagine—and you will never hear the lid jiggle from steam or see the liquids boil. If you have a slow cooker purchased more recently, in the last ten years or so, you are probably used to hearing that lid jiggle from steam—even on low. While we love the first slow cookers (and yes, some of our nostalgic favorites are pictured on page 3), they are now quite rare. Their slow heat is just not suited to baking the cakes or cheesecakes in springform pans like we do in this book. We tested the recipes in slow cookers that are newer and hotter than their antique counterparts, and for the best results, we recommend that you use the newer, hotter models for these recipes.

BAKING A CAKE OR CHEESECAKE

We recommend using a 7-inch springform pan for cakes or cheesecakes— which means that the cake is a perfect size to serve or give as a special gift. That 7-inch-diameter cake is ideal—it makes enough to serve a typical dinner party, yet does not make such a large cake that you have days and days of leftovers. It is also the ideal size to make and give as a gift to welcome a new neighbor, spread holiday joy, cheer an ailing friend, or share with a coworker.

What Is a Springform Pan?

A springform pan is a pan with two parts: a base and an outer ring with a clamp that allows it to expand when released. Thanks to the clamp, the sides of the pan can be lifted off the base of the pan without disturbing whatever you've baked or chilled in the pan. To use a springform pan, tighten the sides so the bottom is held snug, and then fill the pan for baking. Once the cake is cool, gently run a table knife around the edges of the cake, then loosen the clamp and remove the sides. The cake will still rest on the bottom of the pan, but since the sides are gone, it makes it easy and attractive to cut and serve the cake.

Occasionally you may want to remove the cake from the bottom of the pan—especially if you wish to wrap it as a gift or serve it on your own cake plate. We recommend spraying the bottom of the pan with nonstick spray before baking. Occasionally, we will also cut a circle of parchment paper to line the bottom to ensure easy removal.

A springform pan usually clamps so tightly that the bottom and sides are so firmly attached that batter or filling does not seep out while baking. If in doubt, or if your pan does not clamp together tightly, wrap the outside of the bottom and sides of the pan in aluminum foil before filling the pan.

It may take a little effort to buy a 7-inch springform pan. We only occasionally find them at retail kitchen shops or discount merchants, but they are readily available online. We sell them on our site, www.pluggedintocooking.com. Additionally, sites like Amazon.com and other common online retailers sell the correct size pan.

Check the Fit

A 7-inch springform pan is perfectly sized to fit in most larger slow cookers—especially a 5-quart or larger slow cooker. If it fits, you can bake in it, so confirm that it fits down flat and does not rest on the sides of the stoneware bowl. Be sure to check the fit of the springform pan in your slow cooker before starting a recipe.

Place the Springform Pan on an Aluminum Foil Ring

An aluminum foil ring holds the springform pan up, off the bottom of the slow cooker, and lets the warm air encircle it evenly. Crumple a sheet of aluminum foil, about 24 inches long, into a thin strip, then form the strip into a 7-inch ring. Place the foil ring in the bottom of your slow cooker. Center the filled pan evenly on top of the foil ring. Do not cover the top of the springform pan directly with foil; instead, put the lid on the slow cooker.

What About Other Pans?

Occasionally, we use loaf pans to bake in large, oval slow cookers. They work well for cakes but not for cheesecakes. (When baking a cheesecake, you need to use the springform pan so you can remove the sides of the pan to serve the cheesecake.) Select an 8½ x 4½–inch metal loaf pan. Pans without handles are more likely to fit correctly. Be sure to check the fit of the pan in the slow cooker before starting a recipe. Place the filled loaf pan on an aluminum foil ring (see page 6). Do not cover the top of the loaf pan directly with foil; instead, put the lid on the slow cooker.

Parchment Paper Lining

For some puddings and other treats, a parchment paper lining will even out the heat and protect the sides of the dessert from overbrowning. Place a sheet of parchment paper, about 16 x 12 inches, over the stoneware insert of the slow cooker. Press it down so the paper conforms snugly against the bottom and walls of the insert. It is necessary to cover the stoneware completely, so if needed, place a second sheet of parchment paper over the first, perpendicular to the first and crisscrossing the papers. Press the papers down evenly and be sure they line the stoneware bowl snugly. Press carefully so as not to tear the paper. (If it tears, start over so the paper forms a bowl and the liquids from the recipe cannot seep out.) Fold down the top edges of the paper just enough so the lid will rest flat on the stoneware.

REMOVING CAKES FROM THE SLOW COOKER

Carefully remove the hot pan or puddings from the slow cooker. Remember, while slow cookers bake more slowly, they are still hot. Use caution and hot pads to carefully lift the hot pan out of the slow cooker.

MEASURE ACCURATELY TO ACHIEVE SUCCESS

Accurately measuring the ingredients is always the first step toward the best baking. While you might be able to estimate an ingredient when seasoning a soup or stew, baking is a precise science, and you need to measure carefully.

Select the correct equipment to measure accurately.

Dry measuring cups: Dry measuring cups are usually sold as nested 1-, ½-, ⅓-, and ¼-cup measures. It is important to use these when measuring flour, sugar, or other dry ingredients so you can level off the top with a flat edge, such as a table knife.

Liquid measuring cup: This is a clear, marked glass or plastic cup with a spout used to measure liquids. Check the measurement at eye level to be sure it is accurate. Do not measure dry ingredients in this cup—you may be tempted to shake the cup to try to level it off and that will compact the flour and cause incorrect measurements.

Measuring spoons: Measuring spoons are usually sold as nested 1-tablespoon, 1-teaspoon, ½-teaspoon, and ¼-teaspoon measures. Fill the spoon and if measuring a dry ingredient, level it off with the flat edge of a knife. Remember that 3 teaspoons equal 1 tablespoon; if a recipe calls for 1½ tablespoons, measure 1 tablespoon plus 1 teaspoon plus ½ teaspoon.

If measuring a sticky ingredient, like honey, molasses or syrup, peanut butter, or solid shortening, spray the cup or spoon first with nonstick spray. The sticky ingredient will come out of the measuring cup or spoon much more easily.

Other Equipment

Mixer: Many of the recipes recommend using an electric mixer. The recipes are small enough that they work well with a hand mixer—no need to get out the big stand mixer.

Whisk: We often recommend whisking the flour with the leavening ingredients and salt so they are thoroughly blended and aerated before adding them to the liquid ingredients.

Wire rack: Most of the cake recipes recommend transferring the baked cake from the slow cooker to a wire rack to cool.

CHOOSE THE BEST INGREDIENTS

Follow the recipes, using the ingredients listed. Substituting other ingredients, especially those that are labeled "lower fat" or "light," or those ingredients that are formulated for special diets or to avoid specific allergens, may affect the results.

Canola or vegetable oil: There is an array of oils in the baking aisle and most will work well. For baking, choose flavorless, "neutral" oils like canola, corn, or vegetable oil, and save those oils with a distinctive flavor like olive oil or walnut oil for other cooking tasks or when called for in specific recipes. To measure oil, pour it into a liquid measure and check the volume at eye level.

Vegetable shortening: This fat is a solid at room temperature and is essentially flavorless. To measure accurately, fill a dry measuring cup with shortening and press down to eliminate air pockets. You can store vegetable shortening at room temperature for 8 to 12 months.

Flour: We recommend all-purpose flour for many recipes. To measure any kind of flour (all-purpose or whole grain), spoon the flour out of the flour canister and into the dry measuring cup, and then level it off with the flat edge of a table knife. (This is known as the spoon-and-sweep method for measuring.) Do not dip the measuring cup into the flour canister, nor shake the cup to level it off. Flour does not need to be sifted for the recipes in this book. Store all-purpose flour in an airtight container at room temperature for 6 to 8 months. Store whole-grain flour in an airtight container in the refrigerator for up to 6 months, or in the freezer for up to 1 year.

Brown sugar: Brown sugar is labeled dark or light, and you can use them interchangeably in this book. The dark brown version has a more intense molasses flavor and is popular in Southern cooking. We find people often use the one they are most familiar with, which is frequently the one they grew up with—so Roxanne chooses dark and Kathy chooses light. Brown sugar is always measured "packed," so spoon it into the measuring cup and pack it lightly to remove any air pockets. It should hold its shape when turned out into the mixing bowl.

Sugar: We tested the recipes in this book with sugar. These recipes were not tested with other sweeteners, and the use of sweeteners may affect the results. To measure sugar, fill a dry measuring cup to overflowing, and then level it off with the flat edge of a table knife.

Salt: There is now an array of salts available—different colors, origins, and textures. While we may turn to these for savory cooking, typical table salt is our choice for baking.

Butter: We prefer unsalted or "sweet" butter for baking, and it is the butter used in the recipes in this book. We do not recommend using margarine. When cooking, it is difficult to substitute "light" butter or butter spreads, as they have a higher moisture content than regular butter and will affect the texture and flavor of the baked good or dish. Purchase butter when it's on sale, then store it in the freezer for 6 to 9 months.

Eggs: The recipes in this book were tested using large eggs. Results will not be consistent if you use medium or jumbo eggs, or egg substitutes.

Leavening agents: Baking soda and baking powder are the chemicals that make cakes rise—without them, your baked goods could end up dense and heavy. Using a little baking soda or baking powder—or both—creates a light and wonderful cake. Baking soda reacts with acids, like vinegar, fruit juice, or buttermilk. Baking powder does not require an acid, so you will often see it used in cakes made with milk. Do not interchange baking powder with baking soda. Both can be stored in an airtight container at room temperature. Store baking powder for up to 18 months and baking soda for up to about 2 years.

Milk: Milk is often used in cakes, puddings, and many other desserts. For optimum flavor, use regular whole dairy milk, but in a pinch, 2 percent or reduced-fat milk can be used.

Buttermilk: We love the tang and flavor of buttermilk. The acidity of buttermilk also affects leavening, so you cannot substitute milk for buttermilk. If you are in a pinch and don't have buttermilk on hand, pour 1 tablespoon white vinegar or lemon juice into a 1-cup measure and add milk to equal 1 cup. Allow it to stand for a few minutes, then measure out the volume you need for the recipe you are preparing.

Cream: Heavy or whipping cream gives a great flavor and is a common ingredient in cheesecakes and fondue. Whipped, it is the ideal topping on warm cobblers, crisps, and other desserts. Heavy cream has a fat content of 36 to 42 percent—a fact that makes it taste luscious and whip beautifully. Half-and-half, a commercial blend of cream and milk, is used in some recipes. Half-and-half and heavy cream are not interchangeable. Look for both in the dairy section of the grocery store.

To make whipped cream, pour very cold cream into a deep, chilled bowl. Beat with an electric mixer, starting at low speed, then gradually increasing the speed to medium-high until the cream is frothy, then beat until stiff peaks form—the cream should hold its shape when you lift the beaters out of the bowl. Heavy cream doubles in volume when whipped.

If you wish to make a sweetened whipped cream, beat the cream until soft peaks form, and then gradually add confectioners' sugar while beating the cream until it is stiff. Begin with about 2 tablespoons confectioners' sugar to each 1 cup cream, or sweeten to taste.

Chocolate: The array of baking chocolate has exploded, with many varieties, origins, and artisanal products now available at the local grocery store. Common baking chocolate bars include unsweetened, semisweet, and bittersweet chocolate, while chips are now available in such flavors as semisweet and milk chocolate. Each variety has a slightly different flavor and level of sweetness, but we find that in our recipes you can generally substitute one variety of baking chocolate for another. Candy bars, on the other hand, are usually much sweeter, so we do not recommend substituting a chocolate candy bar for the baking chocolate. If a candy bar is to be used, it will be specified in the recipe.

Now, get ready to bake great desserts in your slow cooker!

We are passionate about slow cooker desserts and are thrilled you are sharing this sweet journey with us. Slow cookers have always been a part of both our professional life and our friendship. We met in the test kitchen of Rival, the company that first introduced the slow cooker to the world, and used cakes, like the Harvey Wallbanger and Sherry Pecan, to test how evenly new models of slow cookers heated. Company engineers, sales professionals, and marketing reps came into the test kitchen daily for sweet nibbles!

Now fast-forward some thirty years, and we are still the best of friends and still love the moist, wonderful cakes that can only be baked in a slow cooker. Today's slow cooker recipes feature new flavors and up-to-date ingredients, and they are baked in new, sleek models of the popular appliance—but the rich, wonderful flavor is still there.

We hope you enjoy these flavorful slow cooker desserts as much as we have enjoyed sharing our favorite recipes with you.

CHEESECAKES

HOW THE COOKIE CRUMBLES CHEESECAKE

MAKES 1 (7-INCH) CHEESECAKE • SLOW COOKER SIZE: 5 QUART OR LARGER

The name says it all—after one heavenly bite, it may quickly become one of your all-time favorite desserts. Rich and creamy cheesecake with a luscious chocolate topping and chocolate cookie crust make this a classic, unbeatable dessert.

CRUST:

Nonstick cooking spray

11 cream-filled chocolate sandwich cookies

2 tablespoons unsalted butter, melted

2 tablespoons sugar

FILLING:

2 (8-ounce) packages cream cheese, at room temperature

⅔ cup sugar

2 large eggs, at room temperature

3 tablespoons heavy cream

1 tablespoon all-purpose flour

1 teaspoon pure vanilla extract

GANACHE:

½ cup semisweet chocolate chips

¼ cup heavy cream

2 tablespoons unsalted butter

½ teaspoon pure vanilla extract

2 teaspoons confectioners' sugar

MAKE THE CRUST: Preheat the oven to 375°F. Spray the bottom of a 7-inch springform pan with nonstick spray. Crumple a sheet of aluminum foil, about 24 inches long, into a thin strip, then form it into a 7-inch ring. Place the ring in the bottom of a large slow cooker.

Place the cookies in the work bowl of a food processor. Pulse to make fine crumbs. Remove ⅓ cup of the cookie crumbs and set aside. Add the melted butter and sugar to the crumbs in the food processor and pulse to combine. Pour the crumb mixture into the prepared pan. Press the crumbs evenly across the bottom of pan. Bake in the oven for 5 minutes, or until the crust is set. Let cool on a wire rack.

MAKE THE FILLING: In a large bowl using a hand mixer, beat together the cream cheese and sugar on medium-high speed until the mixture is light and fluffy. Add the eggs one at a time, beating well after each addition. Beat in the heavy cream, flour, and vanilla. Pour half the filling over the cooled crust. Sprinkle with the reserved ⅓ cup cookie crumbs. Top with remaining filling.

Place the filled springform pan on the foil ring in the slow cooker. Cover the slow cooker and bake on high for 2½ to 3 hours, or until the filling has softly set. Unplug the slow cooker; do not remove the cheesecake. Let the cheesecake cool in the slow cooker for 1 to 2 hours, then remove the cheesecake from the slow cooker and let cool completely on a wire rack.

MAKE THE GANACHE: Place the chocolate chips in a small bowl and set aside. Place the heavy cream and butter in a microwave-safe glass 1-cup measure. Microwave on high for 25 to 35 seconds, or until the cream is hot and the butter is beginning to melt. Stir to finish melting the butter, if necessary. Pour the mixture over the chocolate chips. Using a small whisk, whisk until the chocolate has melted and the mixture is smooth and well combined. Add the vanilla and confectioners' sugar and continue whisking until smooth.

Pour the ganache over the cooled cheesecake. Refrigerate the cheesecake for at least 4 hours or overnight before serving.

TIPS:

- **Cheesecakes should be stored in the refrigerator until serving time and should not be allowed to sit out at room temperature for longer than 2 hours.**

- **Springform pans make serving the cheesecake easy and attractive. Refrigerate the cheesecake until it is well chilled, then remove the sides of the pan for serving.**

BROWNIE CHUNK CHEESECAKE

MAKES 1 (7-INCH) CHEESECAKE • SLOW COOKER SIZE: 5 QUART OR LARGER

Roxanne's husband, Bob Bateman, adores brownies. It seems only natural to incorporate his favorite dessert into a creamy, rich cheesecake. Birthday cakes take on a new meaning at her house, as this is always the version he selects.

CRUST:

Nonstick cooking spray

7 cream-filled chocolate sandwich cookies

1 tablespoon unsalted butter, melted

2 tablespoons sugar

FILLING:

2 (8-ounce) packages cream cheese, at room temperature

1 cup sugar

3 large eggs, at room temperature

¼ cup heavy cream

1 tablespoon all-purpose flour

1 teaspoon pure vanilla extract

1½ cups brownie cubes (see Tips)

GANACHE:

½ cup semisweet chocolate chips

¼ cup heavy cream

2 tablespoons unsalted butter

½ teaspoon pure vanilla extract

2 teaspoons confectioners' sugar

MAKE THE CRUST: Preheat the oven to 375°F. Spray the bottom of a 7-inch springform pan with nonstick spray. Crumple a sheet of aluminum foil, about 24 inches long, into a thin strip, then form it into a 7-inch ring. Place the ring in the bottom of a large slow cooker.

Place the cookies in the work bowl of a food processor. Pulse to make fine crumbs. Add the melted butter and sugar and pulse to combine. Pour the crumb mixture into the prepared pan. Press the crumbs evenly across the bottom of pan. Bake in the oven for 5 minutes, or until the crust is set. Let cool on a wire rack.

MAKE THE FILLING: In a large bowl using a hand mixer, beat together the cream cheese and sugar on medium speed until the mixture is light and fluffy. Add the eggs one at a time, beating well after each addition. Beat in the heavy cream, flour, and vanilla. Using a spatula, gently fold in the brownie cubes. Pour the filling over the cooled crust.

Place the filled springform pan on the foil ring in the slow cooker. Cover the slow cooker and bake on high for 2½ to 3 hours, or until the filling has softly set. Unplug the slow cooker; do not remove the cheesecake. Let the cheesecake cool in the slow cooker for 1 to 2 hours, then remove the cheesecake from the slow cooker and let cool completely on a wire rack.

MAKE THE GANACHE: Place the chocolate chips in a small bowl and set aside. Place the heavy cream and butter in a microwave-safe glass 1-cup measure. Microwave on high for 25 to 35 seconds, or until the cream is hot and the butter is beginning to melt. Stir to finish melting the butter, if necessary. Pour the mixture over the chocolate chips. Using a small whisk, whisk until the chocolate has melted and the mixture is smooth and well combined. Add the vanilla and confectioners' sugar and continue whisking until smooth.

Pour the ganache over the cooled cheesecake. Refrigerate the cheesecake for at least 4 hours or overnight before serving.

TIPS:

- **Use your own preference on the size of the brownie cubes. Some people prefer bite-size cubes, while others like larger pieces that require a fork to enjoy. There is no wrong size.**

- **Don't let a lack of baked brownies prevent you from trying this recipe. You can easily purchase brownie bites or premade brownies from the bakery section of your grocery store.**

- **For added fun, reserve a few brownie bites and cut them into smaller cubes. Sprinkle the small cubes over the ganache.**

STRAWBERRY DAIQUIRI CHEESECAKE

MAKES 1 (7-INCH) CHEESECAKE • SLOW COOKER SIZE: 5 QUART OR LARGER

We can thank Cuban bartenders for inventing mojitos and daiquiris. Life really has never been the same since. In this recipe, strawberries, rum, and liqueur combine to make a prizewinning dessert.

CRUST:

Nonstick cooking spray

⅔ cup graham cracker crumbs

2 tablespoons finely chopped pecans

2 tablespoons sugar

2 tablespoons unsalted butter, melted

GLAZE:

2 tablespoons cornstarch

1 (12-ounce) jar strawberry preserves

2 tablespoons orange-flavored liqueur

Red food coloring (optional)

FILLING:

2 (8-ounce) packages cream cheese, at room temperature

⅔ cup sugar

2 large eggs, at room temperature

1½ tablespoons all-purpose flour

⅔ cup sour cream

¼ cup light rum

3 tablespoons fresh lime juice

½ teaspoon pure vanilla extract

GARNISH:

6 to 10 fresh strawberries, sliced (optional)

MAKE THE CRUST: Preheat the oven to 375°F. Spray the bottom of a 7-inch springform pan with nonstick spray. Crumple a sheet of aluminum foil, about 24 inches long, into a thin strip, then form it into a 7-inch ring. Place the ring in the bottom of a large slow cooker.

In a medium bowl, combine the graham cracker crumbs, pecans, sugar, and melted butter. Stir well. Press the mixture into the prepared pan, pressing it over the bottom and up the sides by about ½ inch. Bake in the oven for 5 to 7 minutes, or until the crust is set. Let cool on a wire rack.

MAKE THE GLAZE: In a small saucepan, combine the cornstarch and ¼ cup water and stir until smooth. Add the preserves and heat the mixture over medium heat, stirring continuously, until the preserves have melted and the mixture has thickened. Remove from the heat and add the liqueur; blend well. If desired, add a few drops of red food coloring for a vibrant red color. Set aside to cool.

MAKE THE FILLING: In a large bowl using a hand mixer, beat together the cream cheese and sugar on medium-high speed, until the mixture is light and fluffy. Add the eggs one at a time, beating well after each addition. Beat in the flour, sour cream, rum, lime juice, and vanilla. Pour half of the filling over the cooled crust. Drizzle 4 tablespoons of the glaze over the filling, then top with the remaining cheesecake filling.

Place the filled springform pan on the foil ring in the slow cooker. Cover the slow cooker and bake on high for 2½ to 3½

hours, or until the filling has just set. (The center may jiggle but will continue to cook while cooling.) Unplug the slow cooker; do not remove the cheesecake. Let the cheesecake cool in the covered slow cooker for 1 to 2 hours, then remove the cheesecake from the slow cooker and let cool completely on a wire rack.

Carefully spread the remaining glaze over the cooled cheesecake. Refrigerate the cheesecake for at least 4 hours or overnight. If desired, before serving, top the glaze with sliced fresh strawberries.

TIPS:

- For a variation on serving, do not spread the glaze over the cooled cheesecake, but serve it as a sauce on the side. If desired, add 1 to 1½ cups sliced fresh strawberries to the sauce.

- Cheesecakes freeze beautifully, so bake them ahead as desserts and gifts, especially during the busy holiday season. To freeze, bake the cheesecake as directed but omit the fresh fruit glaze, whipped cream, or chocolate ganache topping. Chill the cheesecake, seal it in an airtight freezer bag, and freeze for up to 2 months. When ready to serve, thaw it overnight in the refrigerator, then garnish or top as desired, and serve.

- Why let the cheesecake cool in the slow cooker? The cheesecake finishes baking, without overbaking. More important, cheesecakes need to cool slowly so the surface does not crack, and the best way to do this is to let the slow cooker and the cheesecake cool together.

GERMAN CHOCOLATE CHEESECAKE

MAKES 1 (7-INCH) CHEESECAKE • SLOW COOKER SIZE: 5 QUART OR LARGER

No need to fuss with layers of cake when you want to enjoy the flavor and elegance of German choco-late. Prepare this cheesecake and your guests will think you spent hours in the kitchen. . . . Shhh! Don't tell!

CRUST:

Nonstick cooking spray

7 cream-filled chocolate sandwich cookies

2 tablespoons unsalted butter, melted

2 tablespoons sugar

FILLING:

4 ounces semisweet chocolate, chopped

2 (8-ounce) packages cream cheese, at room temperature

⅔ cup sugar

Pinch of salt

2 large eggs, at room temperature

¼ cup sour cream

1 tablespoon all-purpose flour

2 tablespoons unsweetened cocoa powder

1 teaspoon pure vanilla extract

Pecan and Coconut Frosting (page 62)

MAKE THE CRUST: Preheat the oven to 375°F. Spray the bottom of a 7-inch springform pan with nonstick spray. Crumple a sheet of aluminum foil, about 24 inches long, into a thin strip, then form it into a 7-inch ring. Place the ring in the bottom of a large slow cooker.

Place the cookies in the work bowl of a food processor. Pulse to make fine crumbs. Add the melted butter and sugar and pulse to combine. Pour the crumb mixture into the pre-pared pan. Press the crumbs evenly across the bottom of the pan. Bake in the oven for 5 to 7 minutes, or until the crust is set. Let cool on a wire rack.

MAKE THE FILLING: Place the chocolate in a microwave-safe 2-cup glass bowl and microwave on medium (50 percent) power for 1 to 2 minutes, stirring every 30 seconds, or until melted. Set aside.

In a large bowl using a hand mixer, beat together the cream cheese, sugar, and salt on medium-high speed, until the mix-ture is light and fluffy. Add the eggs one at a time, beating well after each addition. Add the sour cream, flour, cocoa powder, and vanilla and beat until smooth. Blend in the melted choco-late. Pour the filling over the cooled crust.

Place the filled springform pan on the foil ring in the slow cooker. Cover the slow cooker and bake on high for 2 to 3 hours, or until the filling has softly set. Unplug the slow cooker; do not remove the cheesecake. Let the cheesecake cool in the covered slow cooker for 1 to 2 hours, then remove the cheesecake from the slow cooker and let cool completely on a wire rack.

Spread the frosting over the top of the cooled cheesecake. Refrigerate the cheesecake for at least 4 hours or overnight before serving.

TIP:

- **If desired, omit the Pecan and Coconut Frosting and serve this cheesecake with a dollop of sweetened whipped cream. Of course, you won't be able to call it German chocolate, but you are sure to enjoy it just the same.**

KEY LIME CHEESECAKE

MAKES 1 (7-INCH) CHEESECAKE • SLOW COOKER SIZE: 5 QUART OR LARGER

Key lime pie is known as the official dessert of the Florida Keys. Thank goodness key lime desserts have flourished and stood the test of time. We prefer the creamy tart flavor of this cheesecake to the tangy flavor of key lime pie.

CRUST:

Nonstick cooking spray

⅔ cup graham cracker crumbs

2 tablespoons sugar

½ teaspoon ground cinnamon

2 tablespoons unsalted butter, melted

FILLING:

8 key limes, or 5 limes, plus more as needed

2 (8-ounce) packages cream cheese, at room temperature

⅔ cup sugar

2 large eggs, at room temperature

1 teaspoon pure vanilla extract

1 tablespoon all-purpose flour

1 cup sour cream

TOPPING

1½ cups heavy cream

3 tablespoons confectioners' sugar

Lime zest, for garnish

MAKE THE CRUST: Preheat the oven to 375°F. Spray the bottom of a 7-inch springform pan with nonstick spray. Crumple a sheet of aluminum foil, about 24 inches long, into a thin strip, then form it into a 7-inch ring. Place the ring in the bottom of a large slow cooker.

In a medium bowl, combine the graham cracker crumbs, sugar, cinnamon, and butter and stir to blend. Press the mixture into the prepared pan. Bake in the oven for 5 to 7 minutes, or until the crust is set. Let cool on a wire rack.

MAKE THE FILLING: Grate the zest from all the limes and set aside. Use a juicing reamer or a hand juicer to juice the limes into a glass measuring cup. If need be, juice more limes to equal ⅓ cup plus 2 tablespoons lime juice. Set aside.

In a large bowl using a hand mixer, beat together the cream cheese and sugar on medium-high speed until light and fluffy. Add the eggs one at a time, beating well after each addition. Beat in the vanilla, flour, sour cream, lime zest, and lime juice. Pour the filling over the cooled crust.

Place the filled springform pan on the foil ring in the slow cooker. Cover the slow cooker and bake on high for 2½ to 3 hours, or until the filling is softly set. Unplug the slow cooker; do not remove the cheesecake. Let the cheesecake cool in the covered slow cooker for 1 to 2 hours, then remove the cheesecake from the slow cooker and let cool completely on a wire rack.

Refrigerate the cheesecake for at least 4 hours or overnight.

MAKE THE TOPPING: When ready to serve, in a large chilled bowl using a hand mixer, whip the heavy cream on medium-high to high speed until frothy. Gradually add the confectioners' sugar and beat until stiff peaks form.

Cut the cheesecake into wedges. Dollop whipped cream on each serving and sprinkle with lime zest.

TIPS:

- **Key limes are smaller and a bit more sharp in flavor than the Persian (standard) limes you typically see at the grocery store. If you prefer the tangy flavor of a key lime, but key limes are not available at your grocery store, use 4 limes and 1 lemon for this recipe.**

- **Key lime juice is available in bottles, however, we do not recommend using bottled key lime juice for this recipe. If you cannot find key limes, use Persian (standard) limes.**

CANDY BAR CHEESECAKE

MAKES 1 (7-INCH) CHEESECAKE • SLOW COOKER SIZE: 5 QUART OR LARGER

The superb flavor of this cheesecake is accented with peanuts, caramel, and chocolate. You will think you are biting into a candy bar!

CRUST:

Nonstick cooking spray

6 cream-filled chocolate sandwich cookies

¼ cup salted roasted peanuts

2 tablespoons unsalted butter, melted

FILLING AND TOPPING:

2 (8-ounce) packages cream cheese, at room temperature

1 (14-ounce) can sweetened condensed milk

2 large eggs, at room temperature

2 tablespoons all-purpose flour

2 teaspoons pure vanilla extract

10 soft caramels, unwrapped

2 ounces semisweet chocolate

¼ cup salted roasted peanuts, chopped

MAKE THE CRUST: Preheat the oven to 375°F. Spray the bottom of a 7-inch springform pan with nonstick spray. Crumple a sheet of aluminum foil, about 24 inches long, into a thin strip, then form it into a 7-inch ring. Place the ring in the bottom of a large slow cooker.

Place the cookies and the peanuts in the work bowl of a food processor. Pulse to finely chop. Add the melted butter and pulse to combine. Press the crumb mixture evenly across the bottom of the prepared pan. Bake in the oven for 5 minutes, or until the crust is set. Let cool on a wire rack.

MAKE THE FILLING: In a large bowl using a hand mixer, beat the cream cheese on medium speed until smooth and blended. Beat in ⅔ cup of the condensed milk; cover and refrigerate the remaining condensed milk. Add the eggs one at a time, beating well after each addition. Beat in the flour and vanilla. Pour the filling over the cooled crust.

Place the filled springform pan on the foil ring in the slow cooker. Cover the slow cooker and bake on high for 2½ to 3 hours, or until the filling is set. Unplug the slow cooker; do not remove the cheesecake. Let the cheesecake cool in the covered slow cooker for 1 to 2 hours, then remove the cheesecake from the slow cooker and let cool completely on a wire rack. Refrigerate cheesecake for at least 4 hours or overnight.

When ready to serve, combine the remaining ⅔ cup condensed milk, the caramels, and the chocolate in a small microwave-safe 2-cup glass bowl. Microwave on high (100 percent) power for 2 minutes, stirring midway through, until hot and melted. Stir until smooth. Let cool for 5 minutes, then drizzle the topping over the cheesecake. Garnish with chopped peanuts.

COCONUT CREAM CHEESECAKE

MAKES 1 (7-INCH) CHEESECAKE • SLOW COOKER SIZE: 5 QUART OR LARGER

The old-fashioned creamy goodness of a coconut cream pie has been captured and intensified in this cheesecake.

CRUST:

Nonstick cooking spray

12 vanilla wafers

2 tablespoons unsalted butter, melted

½ cup sweetened flaked coconut, toasted (see Tips)

FILLING:

2 (8-ounce) packages cream cheese, at room temperature

⅔ cup sugar

2 large eggs, at room temperature

6 tablespoons cream of coconut (see Tips)

2 tablespoons heavy cream

1 tablespoon all-purpose flour

½ teaspoon coconut or vanilla extract

Sweetened whipped cream, for serving (see Tips)

Toasted sweetened flaked coconut, for garnish

MAKE THE CRUST: Preheat the oven to 375°F. Spray the bottom of a 7-inch springform pan with nonstick spray. Crumple a sheet of aluminum foil, about 24 inches long, into a thin strip, then form it into a 7-inch ring. Place the ring in the bottom of a large slow cooker.

Place the cookies in the work bowl of a food processor. Pulse to make fine crumbs. Add the melted butter and toasted coconut and pulse to combine. Press the crumb mixture evenly across the bottom of the prepared pan. Bake in the oven for 5 minutes, or until the crust is set. Let cool on a wire rack.

MAKE THE FILLING: In a large bowl using an electric mixer, beat together the cream cheese and sugar on medium-high speed until light and fluffy. Add the eggs one at a time, beating well after each addition. Beat in the cream of coconut, heavy cream, flour, and coconut extract. Pour the filling over the cooled crust.

Place the filled springform pan on the foil ring in the slow cooker. Cover the slow cooker and bake on high for 2½ to 3 hours, or until the filling is softly set. Unplug the slow cooker; do not remove the cheesecake. Let the cheesecake cool in the covered slow cooker for 1 to 2 hours, then remove the cheesecake from the slow cooker and let cool completely on a wire rack.

Refrigerate the cheesecake for at least 4 hours or overnight. Just before serving, garnish with whipped cream and toasted coconut.

- Toasting the coconut intensifies the flavor. To toast coconut in the oven, spread sweetened flaked coconut in a thin layer on a rimmed baking sheet. Bake at 300°F for 10 to 15 minutes, stirring every 5 minutes to make sure that the coconut browns evenly. Watch carefully so it does not overbrown or burn.

- Cream of coconut is a sweet, thick, creamy liquid popular for use in cocktails. The cans or bottles are often stocked with liquor or cocktail supplies. Do not be confused or attempt to substitute coconut milk for cream of coconut. Coconut milk is thinner and not sweet, and is available in the Asian food section of most grocery stores.

- To make sweetened whipped cream, whip ½ cup heavy cream in a small bowl with a hand mixer on medium-high speed until soft peaks form. Gradually beat in 1 tablespoon confectioners' sugar. Continue beating until stiff peaks form.

PRALINE-PUMPKIN CHEESECAKE

MAKES 1 (7-INCH) CHEESECAKE • SLOW COOKER SIZE: 5 QUART OR LARGER

Move over, pumpkin pie! Autumn would not be complete without pumpkin desserts, and there can be no finer dessert than this: pumpkin cheesecake topped with a sweet pecan praline topping. It is also the perfect cheesecake to make for holiday gift-giving.

CRUST:

Nonstick cooking spray

½ cup graham cracker crumbs

1 tablespoon unsalted butter, melted

2 tablespoons sugar

FILLING:

2 (8-ounce) packages cream cheese, at room temperature

½ cup sugar

¼ cup packed brown sugar

¾ cup pumpkin puree (see Tips)

2 large eggs, at room temperature

1 tablespoon all-purpose flour

½ teaspoon ground cinnamon

2 tablespoons heavy cream

PRALINE TOPPING:

1 tablespoon unsalted butter

¼ cup packed brown sugar

2 tablespoons heavy cream

½ teaspoon pure vanilla extract

⅓ cup chopped pecans, toasted (see Tips)

MAKE THE CRUST: Preheat the oven to 375°F. Spray the bottom of a 7-inch springform pan with nonstick spray. Crumple a sheet of aluminum foil, about 24 inches long, into a thin strip, then form it into a 7-inch ring. Place the ring in the bottom of a large slow cooker.

In a medium bowl, combine the graham cracker crumbs, melted butter, and sugar and stir to blend. Press the crumb mixture into the prepared pan, pressing it evenly over the bottom and about ½ inch up the sides. Bake in the oven for 5 to 7 minutes, or until the crust is set. Let cool on a wire rack.

MAKE THE FILLING: In a large bowl using a hand mixer, beat together the cream cheese, sugar, and brown sugar on medium-high speed until light and fluffy. Beat in the pumpkin. Add the eggs one at a time, beating well after each addition. Beat in the flour, cinnamon, and heavy cream. Pour the filling over the cooled crust.

Place the filled springform pan on the foil ring in the slow cooker. Cover the slow cooker and bake on high for 2½ to 3 hours, or until the filling is set. Unplug the slow cooker; do not remove the cheesecake. Let the cheesecake cool in the covered slow cooker for 1 to 2 hours, then remove the cheesecake from the slow cooker and let cool completely on a wire rack.

Refrigerate the cheesecake for at least 4 hours or overnight.

MAKE THE PRALINE TOPPING: Place the butter in a microwave-safe 1-cup glass bowl and microwave on high (100 percent) power for 30 to 40 seconds, or until melted. Stir in the brown

sugar. Microwave on high for 30 seconds. Stir well. Microwave for 10 seconds more, or until the sugar has melted and the mixture is bubbling and hot. Stir in the heavy cream, blending well. Microwave on high for 10 seconds, or until the mixture is bubbling and hot. Stir until the sauce is smooth. Stir in the vanilla and pecans. Let the topping cool for about 5 minutes.

Spoon the warm praline topping over the cheesecake.

TIPS:

- **Have leftover canned pumpkin? Refrigerate the pumpkin in an airtight container for up to 1 week, or freeze for up to 3 months. When ready to use, thaw the pumpkin overnight in the refrigerator, then stir well and use as directed in the recipe.**

- **Toasting pecans intensifies their flavor. To toast pecans, spread them in a single layer on a rimmed baking sheet. Bake at 350°F for 5 to 7 minutes, or until lightly toasted, watching carefully to make sure the nuts do not burn.**

S'MORE CHEESECAKE

MAKES 1 (7-INCH) CHEESECAKE • SLOW COOKER SIZE: 5 QUART OR LARGER

There just can't be a campout without s'mores! After many years as a Girl Scout leader, Kathy abides by this rule. When campfires are just not possible, this cheesecake is ideal, as it features all of those same scrumptious flavors.

CRUST:

Nonstick cooking spray

½ cup graham cracker crumbs

2 tablespoons unsalted butter, melted

1 tablespoon sugar

FILLING:

2 (8-ounce) packages cream cheese, at room temperature

⅔ cup packed brown sugar

¼ cup marshmallow creme

2 ounces semisweet chocolate, melted and cooled

3 large eggs, at room temperature

2 tablespoons all-purpose flour

1 teaspoon pure vanilla extract

1 (1.55-ounce) milk chocolate candy bar, chopped

MARSHMALLOW TOPPING:

½ cup heavy cream

¼ cup marshmallow creme

½ teaspoon pure vanilla extract

2 teaspoons graham cracker crumbs, for garnish

MAKE THE CRUST: Preheat the oven to 375°F. Spray the bottom of a 7-inch springform pan with nonstick spray. Crumple a sheet of aluminum foil, about 24 inches long, into a thin strip, then form it into a 7-inch ring. Place the ring in the bottom of a large slow cooker.

In a medium bowl, stir together the graham cracker crumbs, butter, and sugar. Press the crumb mixture evenly across the bottom of the prepared pan. Bake in the oven for 5 minutes, or until the crust is set. Let cool on a wire rack.

MAKE THE FILLING: In a large bowl using a hand mixer, beat the cream cheese on medium-high speed until fluffy. Beat in the brown sugar and marshmallow creme. Beat in the melted chocolate. Add the eggs one at a time, beating well after each addition. Beat in the flour and vanilla.

Spoon half of the filling over the cooled crust. Sprinkle the chopped milk chocolate over the top, then pour over the remaining filling.

Place the filled springform pan on the foil ring in the slow cooker. Cover the slow cooker and bake on high for 2½ to 3 hours, or until the filling has just set. Unplug the slow cooker; do not remove the cheesecake. Let the cheesecake cool in the covered slow cooker for 1 to 2 hours, then remove the cheesecake from the slow cooker and let cool completely on a wire rack.

Refrigerate the cheesecake for at least 4 hours or overnight.

MAKE THE MARSHMALLOW TOPPING: In a small bowl using a hand mixer, beat the heavy cream on medium-high speed until soft peaks form. Add the marshmallow creme and beat until stiff peaks form. Beat in the vanilla.

Pipe or dollop the marshmallow topping on the cheesecake in a decorative fashion. Sprinkle with graham cracker crumbs to garnish.

TIPS:

- **If desired, garnish the cheesecake with chocolate curls. To make chocolate curls, use a vegetable peeler to gently shave the edge of a large chocolate bar.**

- **For over-the-top flavor, just before serving, drizzle the cheesecake with chocolate sauce.**

CAKES
and
FROSTINGS

FRENCH LEMON CAKE WITH LEMON GLAZE

MAKES 1 (7-INCH) ROUND CAKE • SLOW COOKER SIZE: 5 QUART OR LARGER

We fell in love with the moist, soft texture of this cake. It is wonderful with the tart lemon glaze and even better topped with the glaze and fresh blueberries. Be prepared for your friends to request the recipe for themselves.

CAKE:

1¼ cups all-purpose flour

¾ teaspoon baking powder

Dash of salt

½ cup unsalted butter, at room temperature, plus more for the pan

1 cup sugar

1 large egg, at room temperature

½ cup sour cream

Zest of 1 lemon

2 tablespoons fresh lemon juice

½ teaspoon pure vanilla extract

GLAZE:

1 tablespoon fresh lemon juice

½ cup confectioners' sugar

MAKE THE CAKE: Butter a 7-inch springform pan and set aside. Crumple a sheet of aluminum foil, about 24 inches long, into a thin strip, then form it into a 7-inch ring. Place the ring in the bottom of a large slow cooker.

In a medium bowl, whisk together the flour, baking powder, and salt; set aside.

In a large bowl using a hand mixer, beat together the butter and sugar on medium-high speed until light and fluffy. Beat in the egg. Add the sour cream and blend well.

Add the flour mixture to the butter mixture, beating until well blended. Beat in the lemon zest, lemon juice, and vanilla.

Pour the batter into the prepared pan. Place the filled springform pan on the foil ring in the slow cooker. Cover the slow cooker and bake on high for 3 to 4 hours, or until a wooden pick inserted into the center of the cake comes out clean.

Transfer the pan to a wire rack to cool for 10 minutes. Remove the outer ring from the pan and let the cake cool completely.

MAKE THE GLAZE: In a small bowl, whisk together the lemon juice and confectioners' sugar until smooth. Pour the glaze over the cooled cake.

TIP:

- **Lemon zest is easy to grate using a Microplane grater. Remember that the wonderful, intense lemon flavor you want is in the colored portion, but the white pith is bitter.**

NUTMEG CAKE

MAKES 1 (7-INCH) ROUND CAKE • SLOW COOKER SIZE: 5 QUART OR LARGER

Yes, nutmeg is a popular spice, but so often it is masked by other spices like cinnamon and cloves. It's time to let the incredible flavor of nutmeg shine! The flavor of nutmeg is especially good, and it is easy to add.

1¼ cups all-purpose flour, plus more for the pan

1 teaspoon ground nutmeg

¾ teaspoon baking powder

¼ teaspoon baking soda

Dash of salt

¼ cup unsalted butter, at room temperature, plus more for the pan

¾ cup packed brown sugar

1 large egg, at room temperature

½ cup sour cream

½ teaspoon pure vanilla extract

⅓ cup whole milk

Brown Sugar–Pecan Glaze (optional; recipe follows)

Butter and flour a 7-inch springform pan and set aside. Crumple a sheet of aluminum foil, about 24 inches long, into a thin strip, then form it into a 7-inch ring. Place the ring in the bottom of a large slow cooker.

In a medium bowl, whisk together the flour, nutmeg, baking powder, baking soda, and salt; set aside.

In a large bowl using a hand mixer, beat together the butter and brown sugar on medium-high speed until light and fluffy. Beat in the egg. Beat in the sour cream and vanilla.

Add the flour mixture alternately with the milk, in three additions of the flour and two of the milk, beating until smooth after each addition.

Pour the batter into the prepared pan. Place the filled springform pan on the foil ring in the slow cooker. Cover the slow cooker and bake on high for 2½ to 3 hours, or until a wooden pick inserted into the center of the cake comes out clean.

Transfer the pan to a wire rack to cool for 10 minutes. Remove the outer ring from the pan and let the cake cool completely.

If desired, glaze the cake with Brown Sugar–Pecan Glaze.

BROWN SUGAR-PECAN GLAZE

MAKES ABOUT ¾ CUP

¼ cup packed brown sugar

2 tablespoons unsalted butter

2 tablespoons heavy cream

½ teaspoon pure vanilla extract

⅓ cup chopped pecans, toasted (see Tips, page 36)

Place the brown sugar and butter in a small microwave-safe 1-cup glass bowl and microwave on high (100 percent) power for 1 minute, or until the butter has melted. Stir to combine. Stir in the cream and vanilla. Microwave for 30 seconds. Stir in the pecans. Use as directed in the recipe.

TIPS:

- Grating fresh nutmeg is quick and easy and you will find the flavor so much better than what you'd get in a typical jar of ground nutmeg. If you wish, substitute fresh grated nutmeg for the ground nutmeg in this recipe. Find whole nutmeg seeds in the spice section of the grocery store, then grate them as needed using a nutmeg grater or a Microplane.

- This cake is moist and flavorful enough that you do not have to glaze it. Unfrosted, it is the perfect accompaniment to a morning cup of coffee or tea. You could also lightly dust it with confectioners' sugar for an extraordinary dessert.

- This cake works well in an 8½ x 4½-inch loaf pan. Butter and flour the pan. Prepare and bake as directed, placing the filled loaf pan on an aluminum foil ring in a large oval slow cooker. When done, let cool for 10 minutes in the pan on a wire rack, then invert and remove the cake from the pan.

BACK IN THE DAY CARROT CAKE

MAKES 1 (7-INCH) ROUND CAKE • SLOW COOKER SIZE: 5 QUART OR LARGER

This cake is moist, flavorful, and peppered with carrots, pecans, and raisins. This equates to a winner any day of the week. Now why not gild the lily and serve it with Cream Cheese Frosting?

Nonstick cooking spray

1 cup all-purpose flour

1 teaspoon baking powder

½ teaspoon baking soda

1 teaspoon ground cinnamon

½ teaspoon salt

½ cup plus 2 tablespoons canola or vegetable oil

1 cup sugar

2 large eggs, at room temperature

4 medium carrots, grated (about 2¼ cups)

½ cup chopped pecans, toasted (see Tips, page 36)

½ cup raisins

1 teaspoon pure vanilla extract

Cream Cheese Frosting (page 60)

Spray a 7-inch springform pan with nonstick spray. Crumple a sheet of aluminum foil, about 24 inches long, into a thin strip, then form it into a 7-inch ring. Place the ring in the bottom of a large slow cooker.

In a medium bowl, whisk together the flour, baking powder, baking soda, cinnamon, and salt; set aside.

In a large bowl using a hand mixer, beat together the oil and sugar on medium-high speed until light and fluffy. Add the eggs one at a time, beating well after each.

Beat in the dry ingredients, blending until moistened. Stir in the carrots, pecans, raisins, and vanilla.

Pour the batter into the prepared pan. Place the filled springform pan on the foil ring in the slow cooker. Cover the slow cooker and cook on high for 2½ to 3½ hours, or until a wooden pick inserted into the center of the cake comes out clean.

Transfer the pan to a wire rack to cool for 10 minutes. Remove the outer ring from the pan and let the cake cool completely.

Frost the cooled cake with Cream Cheese Frosting.

TIP:

- If desired, split the cake horizontally and fill with Cream Cheese Frosting, then frost the top, or swirl all of the frosting on top for a dramatic presentation. You can also garnish the top of the frosted cake with chopped toasted pecans, or substitute chopped toasted walnuts.

OLD-FASHIONED GINGERBREAD

MAKES 1 (7-INCH) ROUND CAKE • SLOW COOKER SIZE: 5 QUART OR LARGER

If there was a national Gingerbread Lovers Club, Kathy would sign up instantly to be its president. This wonderful gingerbread cake is perfect to serve on a cool fall day—just cut slices from the warm cake and chase away the chill.

1½ cups all-purpose flour, plus more for the pan

¼ cup packed brown sugar

3 tablespoons sugar

1½ teaspoons ground ginger

¾ teaspoon baking soda

½ teaspoon ground cinnamon

¼ teaspoon baking powder

¼ teaspoon ground cloves

Dash of salt

6 tablespoons unsalted butter, melted, plus more for the pan

½ cup buttermilk (see Tips)

½ cup molasses

1 large egg, at room temperature

Butter and flour a 7-inch springform pan. Crumple a sheet of aluminum foil, about 24 inches long, into a thin strip, then form it into a 7-inch ring. Place the ring in the bottom of a large slow cooker.

In a large bowl, whisk together the flour, brown sugar, sugar, ginger, baking soda, cinnamon, baking powder, cloves, and salt; set aside.

In a small bowl, whisk together the melted butter, buttermilk, molasses, and egg. Pour the buttermilk mixture into the flour mixture. Stir until blended.

Pour the batter into the prepared pan. Place the filled springform pan on the foil ring in the slow cooker. Cover the slow cooker and bake on high for 2½ to 3 hours, or until a wooden pick inserted into the center of the cake comes out clean.

Transfer the pan to a wire rack to cool for 10 minutes. Remove the outer ring from the pan. Serve the cake warm or at room temperature.

TIPS:

- The gingerbread works well in an 8½ x 4½-inch loaf pan. Butter and flour the pan. Prepare and bake as directed, placing the filled loaf pan on an aluminum foil ring in a large oval slow cooker. When done, let cool for 10 minutes in the pan, then invert and remove the cake from pan.

- No buttermilk on hand? Stir 1½ teaspoons lemon juice or white vinegar into ½ cup milk. Let stand for 5 to 10 minutes, or until thickened. Proceed with the recipe.

- If desired, stir ½ cup miniature chocolate chips into the batter. Bake as directed.

CINNAMON-FILLED COFFEE CAKE

MAKES 1 (7-INCH) ROUND CAKE • SLOW COOKER SIZE: 5 QUART OR LARGER

Who doesn't love a perfect, moist coffee cake that takes only minutes to prepare? We deliver big time with this recipe. Roxanne likes to invite friends over for coffee in the fall, and since this can easily be made the day before, catching up with old friends is a breeze.

CAKE:

Nonstick cooking spray

1 cup all-purpose flour

1½ teaspoons baking powder

¼ teaspoon salt

½ cup unsalted butter, at room temperature

1 cup sugar

1 large egg, at room temperature

1 cup sour cream

½ teaspoon pure vanilla extract

FILLING:

½ cup sugar

1 tablespoon ground cinnamon

1 cup chopped pecans, toasted (see Tips, page 36)

MAKE THE CAKE: Spray bottom of a 7-inch springform pan with nonstick spray. Crumple a sheet of aluminum foil, about 24 inches long, into a thin strip, then form it into a 7-inch ring. Place the ring in the bottom of a large slow cooker.

In a medium bowl, whisk together the flour, baking powder, and salt; set aside.

In a large bowl using a hand mixer, beat together the butter and sugar on medium-high speed until light and fluffy. Add the egg and beat well. Add the sour cream and vanilla and beat well.

Add the flour mixture to the butter mixture and mix until just blended. Do not overmix.

MAKE THE FILLING: Stir together the filling ingredients in a small bowl.

Pour half of the batter into the prepared pan. Sprinkle with half of the filling mixture. Top with the remaining batter and sprinkle the remaining filling over the top.

Place the filled springform pan on the foil ring in the slow cooker. Cover the slow cooker and bake on high for 3½ to 4½ hours, or until a wooden pick inserted into the center of the cake comes out clean.

Transfer the pan to a wire rack to cool for 10 minutes. Remove the outer ring from the pan. Serve the cake warm or at room temperature.

GRANDMA'S CHOCOLATE CAKE

MAKES 1 (7-INCH) ROUND CAKE • SLOW COOKER SIZE: 5 QUART OR LARGER

No need to drag out the mixer—this old-fashioned cake can be stirred together by hand in no time. The addition of coffee to chocolate cake batter enhances the chocolate flavor. Grandma definitely knew what she was doing!

Nonstick cooking spray

1 cup all-purpose flour

¼ cup unsweetened cocoa powder

1½ teaspoons baking soda

¼ teaspoon salt

¼ cup semisweet chocolate chips

½ cup sugar

⅓ cup canola or vegetable oil

1 large egg, at room temperature

½ cup strong coffee, at room temperature

½ cup buttermilk (see Tips, page 48)

½ teaspoon pure vanilla extract

Chocolate Icing (page 63)

Spray a 7-inch springform pan with nonstick spray. Crumple a sheet of aluminum foil, about 24 inches long, into a thin strip, then form it into a 7-inch ring. Place the ring in the bottom of a large slow cooker.

In a medium bowl, whisk together the flour, cocoa, baking soda, and salt; set aside.

Place the chocolate chips in a microwave-safe 1-cup glass bowl and microwave on high (100 percent) power for 30 seconds. Stir, then continue to microwave in 10-second intervals, if needed, until the chocolate is melted. Do not overcook or the chocolate will harden.

Pour the melted chocolate into a medium bowl. Whisk in the sugar and oil until blended. Add the egg and whisk well.

Combine the coffee, buttermilk, and vanilla in a small bowl.

Add the flour mixture alternately with the coffee-buttermilk mixture to the chocolate batter, making three additions of flour and two of the coffee-buttermilk and blending until smooth after each addition. (You can use a spoon or whisk for this process. No need to use a mixer.)

Pour the batter into the prepared pan. Place the filled springform pan on the foil ring in the slow cooker. Cover the slow cooker and bake on high for 2½ to 3½ hours, or until a wooden pick inserted into the center of the cake comes out clean.

Transfer the pan to a wire rack to cool for 10 minutes. Remove the outer ring from the pan and let the cake cool completely.

When cool, spoon the Chocolate Icing over the cake, allowing it to drizzle down the sides.

NANTUCKET CRANBERRY CAKE

MAKES 1 (7-INCH) ROUND CAKE • SLOW COOKER SIZE: 5 QUART OR LARGER

Deep red cranberries glisten on top of this cake so it is beautiful and tastes great. Yes, serve it for Thanksgiving, but it is so good, you will want to serve it at holiday coffees or teas or for dessert throughout the fall and winter.

1 cup fresh cranberries

⅓ cup chopped pecans, toasted (see Tips, page 36)

¼ cup plus ⅔ cup sugar

¾ cup all-purpose flour

¼ teaspoon baking powder

¼ teaspoon salt

2 large eggs, at room temperature

6 tablespoons unsalted butter, melted, plus more for the pan

½ teaspoon pure vanilla extract

¼ teaspoon pure almond extract

Generously butter the bottom of a 7-inch springform pan. Crumple a sheet of aluminum foil, about 24 inches long, into a thin strip, then form it into a 7-inch ring. Place the ring in the bottom of a large slow cooker.

Arrange the cranberries and pecans evenly over the bottom of the prepared pan. Sprinkle with ¼ cup of the sugar.

In a large bowl, whisk together the remaining ⅔ cup sugar, the flour, baking powder, and salt; set aside.

Whisk the eggs lightly in a small bowl until blended. Stir in the melted butter, vanilla, and almond extract. Stir the butter mixture into the flour mixture until blended. Pour the batter in the pan over the cranberries and pecans.

Place the filled springform pan on the foil ring in the slow cooker. Cover the slow cooker and bake on high for 2½ to 3 hours, or until a wooden pick inserted into the center of the cake comes out clean.

Transfer the pan to a wire rack to cool for 10 minutes, then invert the cake onto a serving plate. Remove the outer ring and bottom of the pan to reveal the cranberries and pecans. Serve warm.

TIPS:

- It is easy to freeze cranberries so you can make this cake all year long. Just place the bag of fresh cranberries into the freezer. Pour out what you need when you are ready to bake the cake and return the remaining cranberries to the freezer. No need to thaw them—just place the cranberries with the pecans in the springform pan and proceed as directed in the recipe.

- A springform pan usually clamps so tightly that the bottom and sides are so firmly attached that the cake batter does not seep out while baking. If in doubt, or if your pan does not clamp together tightly, wrap the outside of the bottom and sides of the pan in aluminum foil before filling the pan.

CIDER-GLAZED APPLE-WALNUT CAKE

MAKES 1 (7-INCH) ROUND CAKE • SLOW COOKER SIZE: 5 QUART OR LARGER

We both grew up near a famous local apple orchard and have fond memories of picking the apples, then rushing home to bake apple cakes and pies. Even if you don't pick them off the tree, be sure to bake this cake on a fall day. It will fill the kitchen with a sweet and spicy aroma, and you will enjoy a wonderful old-fashioned apple cake.

CAKE:

Butter, for the pan

1½ cups all-purpose flour, plus more for the pan

1 cup packed brown sugar

1½ teaspoons baking powder

1 teaspoon ground cinnamon

¼ teaspoon salt

2 large eggs, at room temperature, lightly beaten

¼ cup whole milk

2 tablespoons canola or vegetable oil

1 teaspoon pure vanilla extract

1 firm apple (such as a Braeburn or Granny Smith), peeled, cored, and finely chopped

½ cup chopped walnuts, toasted (see Tips, page 36, for pecans)

GLAZE:

⅓ cup apple cider

1 tablespoon unsalted butter

⅓ cup confectioners' sugar

MAKE THE CAKE: Butter and flour a 7-inch springform pan. Crumple a sheet of aluminum foil, about 24 inches long, into a thin strip, then form it into a 7-inch ring. Place the ring in the bottom of a large slow cooker.

In a large bowl, whisk together the flour, brown sugar, baking powder, cinnamon, and salt; set aside.

In a small bowl, stir together the eggs, milk, oil, and vanilla. Stir the egg mixture into the flour mixture, blending until moistened. (The batter will be thick.) Fold in the apple and walnuts.

Spoon the batter into the prepared pan. Place the filled springform pan on the foil ring in the slow cooker. Cover the slow cooker and bake on high 2½ to 3 hours, or until a wooden pick inserted into the center of the cake comes out clean.

Transfer the pan to a wire rack to cool for 10 minutes. Remove the outer ring from the pan and let the cake cool completely.

MAKE THE GLAZE: Pour the cider into a small saucepan. Bring to a boil, uncovered, over medium-high heat. Reduce the heat to maintain a simmer and cook for 5 to 6 minutes, or until the cider has reduced to about half its original volume. Whisk in the butter. Remove from the heat and whisk in the confectioners' sugar. Let the glaze cool for 5 minutes.

Slowly drizzle the glaze over the cake, allowing it to soak into the cake.

SOUTHERN SWEET POTATO CAKE

MAKES 1 (7-INCH) ROUND CAKE • SLOW COOKER SIZE: 5 QUART OR LARGER

Kathy fell in love with this Southern sweet potato cake many years ago, and it is ideal for the slow cooker. Split and fill the cake with Cream Cheese Frosting and it is a showstopping dessert. It is so good you will want to serve it often, not just at the holidays.

1 cup all-purpose flour, plus more for the pan

½ teaspoon baking soda

½ teaspoon baking powder

½ teaspoon ground cinnamon

½ teaspoon ground nutmeg

¼ teaspoon ground cloves

¼ teaspoon salt

½ cup unsalted butter, at room temperature, plus more for the pan

½ cup sugar

½ cup packed brown sugar

2 large eggs, at room temperature

1 teaspoon pure vanilla extract

1 cup mashed sweet potatoes

Cream Cheese Frosting (page 60)

¼ cup chopped pecans, toasted (see Tips, page 36)

Butter and flour a 7-inch springform pan. Crumple a sheet of aluminum foil, about 24 inches long, into a thin strip, then form it into a 7-inch ring. Place the ring in the bottom of a large slow cooker.

In a medium bowl, whisk together the flour, baking soda, baking powder, cinnamon, nutmeg, cloves, and salt; set aside.

In a large bowl using a hand mixer, beat together the butter, sugar, and brown sugar on medium-high speed until light and fluffy. Add the eggs one at a time, beating well after each addition. Beat in the vanilla. Beat in the sweet potatoes. Add the dry ingredients and beat just until combined.

Pour the batter into the prepared pan. Place the filled springform pan on the foil ring in the slow cooker. Cover the slow cooker and bake on high for 2½ to 3 hours, or until a wooden pick inserted into the center of the cake comes out clean.

Transfer the pan to a wire rack to cool for 10 minutes. Remove the outer ring from the pan and let the cake cool completely.

Frost the cake with the Cream Cheese Frosting. Sprinkle the top with toasted pecans.

TIPS:

- If desired, split the cake horizontally and fill it with Cream Cheese Frosting, then frost the top, or swirl all of the frosting in a dramatic presentation.

- To cook the sweet potatoes, peel and cube 2 medium sweet potatoes. Place them in a saucepan and add cold water to cover; lightly salt the water. Cover and cook over medium heat for 15 to 20 minutes, or until the potatoes are very tender. Drain the potatoes and return them to the pan. Mash with a potato masher until smooth. Measure out 1 cup. If extra mashed potato remains, serve it as an accompaniment for dinner.

- If desired, substitute canned sweet potato puree for the mashed sweet potatoes. You may also use canned sweet potatoes; drain the sweet potatoes well, mash, and proceed as directed in the recipe.

PINEAPPLE BUTTER CAKE

MAKES 1 (7-INCH) ROUND CAKE • SLOW COOKER SIZE: 5 QUART OR LARGER

Buttery goodness combined with sweet pineapple make this cake memorable. All of the flavors of pineapple upside-down cake are hidden inside this wonderful cake.

CAKE:

1½ cups all-purpose flour, plus more for the pan

½ teaspoon baking powder

Dash of salt

¾ cup unsalted butter, at room temperature, plus more for the pan

1 cup sugar

⅓ cup packed brown sugar

3 large eggs, at room temperature

1 (8-ounce) can crushed pineapple in juice, drained, juice reserved

½ teaspoon pure vanilla extract

GLAZE

Reserved pineapple juice, above

1 tablespoon sugar

MAKE THE CAKE: Butter and flour a 7-inch springform pan. Crumple a sheet of aluminum foil, about 24 inches long, into a thin strip, then form it into a 7-inch ring. Place the ring in the bottom of a large slow cooker.

In a medium bowl, whisk together the flour, baking powder, and salt; set aside.

In a large bowl using a hand mixer, beat together the butter, sugar, and brown sugar on medium-high speed until light and fluffy. Add the eggs one at a time, beating well after each addition.

Beat the dry ingredients into the butter mixture. Stir in the crushed pineapple and vanilla.

Pour the batter into the prepared pan. Place the filled springform pan on the foil ring in the slow cooker. Cover the slow cooker and bake on high for 2½ to 3 hours, or until a wooden pick inserted into the center of the cake comes out clean.

Transfer the pan to a wire rack to cool for 10 minutes. Remove the outer ring from the pan and let the cake cool completely.

MAKE THE GLAZE: Pour the reserved pineapple juice into a small saucepan. (It will measure a scant ½ cup.) Bring to a boil, uncovered, over medium heat. Reduce the heat to maintain a simmer and cook for 5 to 6 minutes, or until the juice has reduced to about half its original volume. Stir in the sugar and cook, stirring continuously, for 1 minute.

Drizzle the pineapple glaze over the cooled cake.

- Drain the pineapple well, using the back of a spoon to press lightly on the fruit.

- This cake works well in an 8½ x 4½-inch loaf pan. Butter and flour the pan. Prepare and bake as directed, placing the filled loaf pan on an aluminum foil ring in a large oval slow cooker. When done, let cool for 10 minutes in the pan, then invert and remove the cake from the pan.

CREAM CHEESE FROSTING

MAKES ABOUT 1½ CUPS FROSTING

This sweet, tart, and creamy classic frosting is perfect on so many cakes, especially the Back in the Day Carrot Cake (page 46) and the Southern Sweet Potato Cake (page 56).

4 ounces cream cheese, at room temperature

¼ cup unsalted butter, at room temperature

2¼ cups confectioners' sugar

½ teaspoon pure vanilla extract

In a medium bowl using a hand mixer, beat together the cream cheese and butter on medium-high speed until light and fluffy. Beat in the sugar and vanilla until blended. Use the frosting as directed in the recipe.

TIPS:

- **Do not be tempted to add milk or another liquid to the frosting too early. When you first beat the sugar into the butter and cream cheese mixture, it may appear dry, but if you continue beating, it will come together into a wonderful, creamy frosting. Of course, once you create a creamy frosting, if you prefer it thinner, you can add a tablespoon or two of heavy cream.**

- **Once your cake is frosted with Cream Cheese Frosting, store the cake in the refrigerator.**

PECAN AND COCONUT FROSTING

MAKES ABOUT 1¼ CUPS

While this is perfect for German Chocolate Cheesecake (page 24), think outside the box and add this rich frosting to other desserts and baked puddings.

⅓ cup evaporated milk

¼ cup unsalted butter, cut into pieces

⅓ cup sugar

1 large egg, at room temperature, lightly beaten

½ teaspoon pure vanilla extract

½ cup chopped pecans, toasted (see Tips, page 36)

½ cup sweetened flaked coconut

In a small saucepan, stir together the evaporated milk, butter, sugar, egg, and vanilla. Cook over medium heat, stirring continuously, for 7 minutes.

Stir in the pecans and coconut. Spoon the warm frosting over the cheesecake or cake as directed in the recipe.

CHOCOLATE ICING

MAKES ABOUT ¾ CUP

Old-fashioned goodness is so easy to achieve. You will love this icing on Grandma's Chocolate Cake (page 50).

¼ cup unsalted butter

¼ cup unsweetened cocoa powder

Pinch of salt

1½ cups confectioners' sugar, sifted

½ teaspoon pure vanilla extract

2 to 3 tablespoons whole milk

In a small saucepan, melt the butter over medium heat. Whisk in the cocoa and salt until well blended. Add the sugar and vanilla, then add the milk as needed until the mixture is smooth and flows well.

BREAD
PUDDINGS
and
PUDDINGS

Praline-Pecan Bread Pudding

Cappuccino Bread Pudding

Warm Brownie Pudding

Brioche Bread Pudding with Fresh Fruit

Dulce de Leche Bread Pudding

Sugar and Spice Tapioca Pudding

Crème Caramel

Rice Pudding with Cherries

PRALINE-PECAN BREAD PUDDING

SERVES 6 TO 8 • SLOW COOKER SIZE: 4 QUART

Your guests will find it impossible to resist this Southern-style pecan-and-cinnamon-flavored bread pudding. Serve it with French Quarter Praline Dip (page 118) as a sauce and brew a cup of chicory coffee. Now you and your guests can enjoy the flavors of New Orleans.

Nonstick cooking spray

1 (14-ounce) can sweetened condensed milk

1 (12-ounce) can evaporated milk

3 large eggs, at room temperature

1 teaspoon ground cinnamon

7 to 8 cups cubed cinnamon swirl bread

½ cup pecan pieces, toasted (see Tips, page 36)

Line a 4-quart slow cooker with parchment paper (see page 7). Spray the parchment paper with nonstick spray.

In a large bowl, whisk together the condensed milk, evaporated milk, eggs, and cinnamon.

Add the bread cubes and pecans and stir gently. Pour the mixture into the slow cooker. Cover the slow cooker and bake on low for 2 to 3 hours, or until the pudding is set.

Spoon the warm bread pudding into individual serving bowls.

TIP:

• **Spoon French Quarter Praline Dip (page 118) over individual bread pudding servings for a decadent delight.**

CAPPUCCINO BREAD PUDDING

MAKES 6 TO 8 SERVINGS • SLOW COOKER SIZE: 4 QUART

Do you love to sip cappuccino? Coffee, milk, chocolate, and a touch of coffee-flavored liqueur make a warm and tempting beverage in your cup—and that same combination makes this bread pudding truly wonderful.

Nonstick cooking spray

8 ounces day-old French bread, cut into 1-inch cubes (5½ to 6 cups)

⅓ cup boiling water

1 tablespoon espresso powder

⅓ cup sugar

1 cup whole milk

1 cup half-and-half

4 large eggs, at room temperature

2 tablespoons coffee-flavored liqueur

1 teaspoon pure vanilla extract

1 cup semisweet chocolate chips

Coffee Hard Sauce (optional; recipe follows)

Preheat the oven to 300°F. Line a 4-quart slow cooker with parchment paper (see page 7). Spray the parchment paper with nonstick spray.

Spread the bread cubes in a single layer on a rimmed baking sheet. Bake in the oven for 20 minutes, or until dry and lightly toasted. Let cool.

In a large bowl, stir together the boiling water, espresso powder, and sugar, stirring until the espresso and sugar have dissolved. Whisk in the milk, half-and-half, eggs, liqueur, and vanilla. Add the toasted bread cubes and stir to coat evenly. Stir in the chocolate chips. Pour the mixture into the slow cooker.

Cover the slow cooker and bake on low for 3½ to 4 hours, or until the pudding is just set. Unplug the slow cooker and let stand, covered, for 30 minutes.

Spoon the bread pudding into individual serving dishes and serve warm. Top, if desired, with Coffee Hard Sauce.

TIP:

• **How do you tell if a bread pudding is set? Insert a table knife into the center. If it comes out clean it is set.**

COFFEE HARD SAUCE

MAKES ¾ CUP

6 tablespoons unsalted butter, at room temperature

1 cup confectioners' sugar

1 tablespoon strong coffee, at room temperature

½ teaspoon pure vanilla extract

In a medium bowl using a hand mixer, beat on medium-high speed until fluffy. Add the sugar and beat until creamy. Add the coffee and vanilla and beat until smooth.

Spoon the sauce over the bread pudding as directed in the recipe.

TIPS:

- **What is hard sauce and when to serve it? Hard sauce is an old-fashioned sauce that classically tops plum pudding but is scrumptious on bread pudding and many other fruit desserts. The curious name refers to the fact that once made, it can be refrigerated until firm—so when a spoonful is placed on the warm pudding, the butter-rich sauce melts over the dessert. For the Cappuccino Bread Pudding, coffee is a great flavoring, but rum, brandy, whiskey, liqueurs, or vanilla are a few of the flavors you can substitute for the coffee so the hard sauce complements different desserts.**

- **If desired, spoon the prepared Coffee Hard Sauce onto a sheet of plastic wrap, shaping the hard sauce roughly into a log about 1½ inches in diameter. Roll the log in the plastic wrap, covering the hard sauce completely. Refrigerate for 1 hour or until the sauce forms a firm log. Unwrap and cut the log crosswise into slices about ¾ inch thick. Place a "disc" of the hard sauce on each serving.**

WARM BROWNIE PUDDING

SERVES 6 TO 8 • SLOW COOKER SIZE: 4 QUART

Who doesn't enjoy warm brownies? If you do, this may become your all-time favorite dessert. Ooey, gooey good! This fudgy brownie pudding cake makes its own chocolate sauce as it bakes. For an over-the-top dessert, serve it with a scoop of ice cream.

---

1 tablespoon unsalted butter, softened

1 cup all-purpose flour

¾ cup plus ½ cup sugar, divided

3 tablespoons plus ¼ cup unsweetened cocoa powder

1½ teaspoons baking powder

Dash salt

½ cup whole milk

2 tablespoons canola or vegetable oil

1 teaspoon pure vanilla extract

½ cup packed brown sugar

1½ cups boiling water

Vanilla ice cream, optional

Using the 1 tablespoon butter, generously butter a 4-quart slow cooker.

In a medium bowl, whisk together the flour, ¾ cup sugar, 3 tablespoons cocoa, baking powder, and salt. Stir in the milk, oil, and vanilla; stir until blended. Spoon the batter into the buttered slow cooker.

In another bowl, whisk together the remaining ½ cup sugar, remaining ¼ cup cocoa, brown sugar, and the boiling water. Whisk until the sugar is dissolved, and then pour gently over the batter in the slow cooker. Do not stir.

Cover the slow cooker and bake on high for 2 to 2 ½ hours or until the top is set. Unplug the slow cooker, and let stand, covered, for 30 minutes.

To serve, spoon the warm brownie pudding and sauce into individual dishes and top, if desired, with ice cream.

BRIOCHE BREAD PUDDING WITH FRESH FRUIT

SERVES 6 TO 8 • SLOW COOKER SIZE: 4 QUART

Absolutely divine! That is how we describe this luscious dessert. Brioche is a French bread that is rich and buttery. It is fantastic in this bread pudding, and the dessert becomes irresistible once topped with fresh berries.

BREAD PUDDING:

Nonstick cooking spray

8 ounces brioche bread, cut into 1-inch cubes (5½ to 6 cups)

4 large eggs, at room temperature

¾ cup sugar

2 teaspoons pure vanilla extract

¼ teaspoon salt

2 cups whole milk

2 cups half-and-half

FRUIT TOPPING:

3 cups fresh blueberries, raspberries, blackberries, or sliced strawberries

2 tablespoons sugar

2 tablespoons seedless raspberry or strawberry preserves

MAKE THE BREAD PUDDING: Preheat the oven to 300°F. Line a 4-quart slow cooker with parchment paper (see page 7). Spray the parchment paper with nonstick spray.

Spread the bread cubes in a single layer on a rimmed baking sheet. Bake in the oven for 20 minutes, or until dry and lightly toasted. Let cool.

In a large bowl, whisk together the eggs and sugar. Whisk in the vanilla, salt, milk, and half-and-half. Stir in the toasted bread cubes. Pour the mixture into the slow cooker.

Cover the slow cooker and bake on low for 3 hours, or until the pudding is just set. Unplug the slow cooker and let stand, covered, for 30 minutes.

MAKE THE FRUIT TOPPING: Combine ½ cup of the berries, the sugar, the preserves, and 1½ tablespoons water in a small saucepan. Heat over medium heat, stirring frequently, and pressing lightly on the fruit with the back of the spoon to release juice, for 4 to 5 minutes, or until the sugar has dissolved. Remove from the heat and let cool for 5 minutes. Stir in the remaining 2½ cups berries.

Spoon the warm bread pudding into individual serving bowls and top with the fruit.

TIP:

- **Brioche is slightly sweet and buttery and adds a great flavor to this bread pudding. If brioche is not available, substitute 5½ to 6 cups of cubed day-old challah bread, croissants, or French bread.**

DULCE DE LECHE BREAD PUDDING

SERVES 6 TO 8 • SLOW COOKER SIZE: 4 QUART

One of Kathy's favorite flavors is dulce de leche, *a thick, rich caramel sauce. What could be better than using that delicious caramel in bread pudding?*

Nonstick cooking spray

10 ounces challah bread, cut into 1-inch cubes (6½ to 7 cups)

4 large eggs, at room temperature

1 (14-ounce) can prepared *dulce de leche* (see Tips)

½ cup sugar

2¼ cups whole milk

2 teaspoons pure vanilla extract

Preheat the oven to 300°F. Line a 4-quart slow cooker with parchment paper (see page 7). Spray the parchment paper with nonstick spray.

Spread the bread cubes in a single layer on a rimmed baking sheet. Bake in the oven for 20 minutes, or until dry and lightly toasted. Let cool.

In a large bowl, whisk the eggs until lightly beaten. Whisk in the *dulce de leche* and sugar until well combined and the sauce is almost smooth. Whisk in the milk and vanilla. Stir in the toasted bread cubes, coating them evenly. Pour the mixture into the slow cooker.

Cover the slow cooker and bake on low for 3½ to 4 hours, or until the pudding is just set. Unplug the slow cooker and let stand, covered, for 30 minutes.

Spoon the pudding into individual serving dishes and serve warm.

TIPS:

• If you don't have challah bread, substitute 6½ to 7 cups of bread cubes cut from another egg-rich bread, French bread, or a crusty country loaf.

• For any bread pudding, select loaves without sesame seeds or poppy seeds.

• *Dulce de leche* is now readily available canned or bottled. Look for it in larger grocery stores, shelved with the Latin American foods or with the condensed milk.

SUGAR AND SPICE TAPIOCA PUDDING

SERVES 6 • SLOW COOKER SIZE: 3 TO 4 QUART

Tapioca pudding is similar to rice pudding but much more appealing to some. Tapioca is derived from the cassava plant, which is common throughout Africa. It has been termed by many words such as "fish eye" or "frog eye." Roxanne's mother always refers to tapioca as "frog eyes," which causes many a raised eyebrow at family gatherings.

½ cup large pearl tapioca

Nonstick cooking spray

3 cups whole milk

½ teaspoon ground cinnamon

Dash of ground nutmeg

Pinch of salt

1 large egg, at room temperature

⅓ cup sugar

Place the tapioca in a medium bowl and cover with 3 cups cold water. Let stand overnight and drain.

Spray a 3- or 4-quart slow cooker with nonstick spray. Add the drained tapioca to the slow cooker. Stir in the milk, cinnamon, nutmeg, and salt.

Cover the slow cooker and cook on high for 2 hours, stirring once or twice.

Whisk the egg and sugar together in a medium bowl. Add ⅓ cup of the hot tapioca mixture from the slow cooker, whisking continuously to prevent the egg from curdling. Repeat two more times until you have incorporated at least 1 cup of the hot tapioca into the egg mixture.

Return the sugar and tapioca mixture to the slow cooker and stir. Cover the slow cooker and cook on high for 8 minutes. Stir well. Cook for 8 minutes more, and stir well. Transfer to a glass bowl and immediately cover the surface of the tapioca with plastic wrap. Let cool for 1 hour, and then refrigerate until thoroughly chilled before serving.

CRÈME CARAMEL

SERVES 4 • SLOW COOKER SIZE: 6 QUART, OVAL

Spain has their flan, the traditional custard baked in caramel-coated cups, but if you travel to France, you will find almost every bistro or cafe will offer crème caramel. Since Roxanne has wanted to live in Paris for years, she clamored to develop a French recipe for the slow cooker. The caramel will pour over the custard as it is unmolded and if you close your eyes, you may envision the Eiffel Tower as you savor the smooth, almost velvety dessert.

CARAMEL:

½ cup sugar

CUSTARD:

3 large egg yolks, at room temperature

1½ cups heavy cream

⅓ cup sugar

1½ teaspoons pure vanilla extract

Pour 1 inch of water into a large slow cooker that will hold four (6-ounce) heatproof ramekins or custard cups. Place the ramekins in the slow cooker.

MAKE THE CARAMEL: Pour 2 tablespoons water into a small, heavy saucepan. Add the sugar and stir until dissolved. Cook over medium-high heat, swirling the pan occasionally (do not stir), for 6 to 8 minutes, until the caramel begins to turn amber. Work quickly and divide the caramel evenly among the ramekins. (Be careful, as the caramel will be very hot.)

MAKE THE CUSTARD: In a medium bowl, whisk the egg yolks. Slowly add the cream and sugar. Whisk until the sugar has dissolved. Add the vanilla. Divide the mixture evenly among the ramekins, over the caramel.

Cover the slow cooker and bake on high for 1½ to 2½ hours, or until the custard is set in the center. Using a flexible spatula and hot pads, carefully remove the custard cups from the slow cooker. Let cool slightly, then cover and refrigerate for at least 3 hours or overnight.

Unmold for serving by running a straight-edged knife around the edges of the ramekins. Invert the custards onto a serving plate. Shake gently, if needed, to release them.

TIP:

- **You may have heatproof coffee cups in your cupboards. These can be used in place of ramekins.**

RICE PUDDING WITH CHERRIES

SERVES 6 TO 8 • SLOW COOKER SIZE: 3½ TO 5 QUART

The world of rice pudding always begins with rice simmered in milk. Rice pudding perfection equates to a luscious creaminess and texture. The slow cooker accomplishes all of this with ease. Adding dried cherries is a pleasant surprise.

Butter, for the slow cooker

5 cups milk

1 cup uncooked Arborio rice

⅔ cup sugar

1 tablespoon pure vanilla extract

½ teaspoon ground cinnamon

¼ teaspoon ground nutmeg

Pinch of salt

⅔ cup dried cherries

Lightly butter a medium slow cooker. Place all the ingredients in the slow cooker; stir to combine.

Cover the slow cooker and cook on low for 3 to 3½ hours, or until the pudding is thick and creamy. Stir well before serving. Serve warm or cold.

TIPS:

- Rice pudding in a slow cooker seems to go from not done, with firm rice and a liquid appearance, to perfectly cooked rice in a thick, rich sauce in a matter of moments. Check the cooking progress every 15 minutes toward the end of the cooking time so you do not overcook.

- If desired, omit the dried cherries and substitute fresh cherries or raisins.

FRUITS

Farmhouse Peach Crisp

Cherry-Rhubarb Crisp

Whole Apple Crisp

Peach and Mango Cobbler

Bananas Foster

Plum-Orange Brown Betty

Blueberry-Almond Buckle

Wine-Poached Pears with Butterscotch Sauce

Cinnamon-Calvados Applesauce

Cherry Clafoutis

Apple Butter

Inside-Out Caramel Apples

Peach Butter

Brandied Peach Jubilee

Candied Cranberry and Crystallized Ginger Chutney

FARMHOUSE PEACH CRISP

SERVES 6 · SLOW COOKER SIZE: 4 QUART

Peach crisp is a mainstay in our homes. We both were born in Missouri, and while Georgia may claim bragging rights to peaches, you haven't lived until you have tasted ripe, juicy peaches from the Show Me state. We are happy to show you success! No worries, though—any fresh, juicy peaches can easily be substituted for Missouri-grown peaches.

Butter or nonstick cooking spray, for the slow cooker

½ cup packed brown sugar

¼ cup sugar

1 cup plus 2 tablespoons all-purpose flour

½ teaspoon baking powder

½ teaspoon ground cinnamon

½ teaspoon ground nutmeg

¼ teaspoon salt

¼ cup unsalted butter, cut into small pieces and chilled

½ cup pecan pieces, toasted (see Tips, page 36)

8 cups sliced peeled fresh peaches

Juice of 1 lemon (about 2 tablespoons)

Vanilla ice cream, for serving

Butter a 4-quart slow cooker or spray it with nonstick spray.

In a medium bowl, combine the brown sugar, sugar, 1 cup of the flour, the baking powder, cinnamon, nutmeg, and salt. Cut in the butter with a pastry cutter or two knives until it forms coarse, even crumbs. Stir in the pecans; set aside.

Place the peaches in the slow cooker and toss with the lemon juice. Sprinkle the remaining 2 tablespoons flour over the peaches and toss lightly.

Gently stir in half of the sugar-pecan mixture. Sprinkle the remaining mixture evenly on top of the peaches.

Cover the slow cooker and bake on low for 2½ to 3½ hours, or until the topping is melted and the peaches are tender. Serve warm, with a scoop of vanilla ice cream.

TIPS:

- **If you are craving peach crisp in the dead of winter, go ahead and substitute frozen peaches for fresh.**

- **For a fun serving idea, ladle servings of Farmhouse Peach Crisp into individual serving bowls or individual cast-iron skillets. Top each serving with ice cream.**

CHERRY-RHUBARB CRISP

SERVES 6 • SLOW COOKER SIZE: 4 QUART

Rhubarb is one of Roxanne's favorites. While she enjoys strawberry rhubarb pies and crisps, replacing strawberries with dark, sweet cherries was a winner!

Nonstick cooking spray

1 (12-ounce) bag frozen unsweetened dark sweet cherries

3 cups sliced rhubarb, cut about ½ inch thick

2 tablespoons quick-cooking tapioca

½ cup sugar

1¼ cups old-fashioned oats

3 tablespoons all-purpose flour

½ cup packed brown sugar

½ teaspoon ground cinnamon

¼ teaspoon salt

¼ cup unsalted butter, cut into small pieces and chilled

Spray a 4-quart slow cooker with nonstick spray.

Combine the cherries, rhubarb, tapioca, and sugar in the slow cooker.

In a medium bowl, combine the oats, flour, brown sugar, cinnamon, and salt. Cut in the butter with a pastry cutter or two knives until it forms coarse, even crumbs. Pour the oat mixture evenly over the rhubarb mixture in the slow cooker.

Cover the slow cooker and bake on high for 2 to 2½ hours, or until the crisp is cooked and the mixture is bubbling. Serve warm.

TIPS:

- **Serve with a scoop of ice cream.**

- **Fresh rhubarb is especially good, and many grocery stores and markets sell it in the spring when it is plentiful. If you cannot find fresh, substitute frozen; no need to thaw it before using.**

- **If you are lucky enough to have a farmers' market that has late-season rhubarb and fresh, sweet cherries at the same time, by all means, use fresh, pitted cherries.**

WHOLE APPLE CRISP

SERVES 6 · SLOW COOKER SIZE: 5 QUART OR LARGER

If old-fashioned baked apples crossed paths with apple crisp, what would you get? This scrumptious recipe is the answer, for it features the best of both of those recipes—whole apples baked to perfection and topped with a sweet, crisp crust.

Nonstick cooking spray

6 medium apples (see Tips)

2 tablespoons fresh lemon juice

¾ cup old-fashioned oats

½ cup packed brown sugar

2 tablespoons all-purpose flour

1 teaspoon ground cinnamon

¼ cup unsalted butter, cut into small pieces and chilled

½ cup chopped walnuts, toasted (see Tips, page 36)

¼ cup pure maple syrup

Spray a large slow cooker with nonstick spray.

Use an apple corer to core the apples, carefully scraping out the seeds and core, but taking care to not cut through the bottom of the apple.

Place the apples upright in the slow cooker, arranging them tightly so their sides touch. Brush the apples with the lemon juice. Drizzle 2 tablespoons water around the apples.

In a medium bowl, stir together the oats, brown sugar, flour, and cinnamon. Cut in the butter with a pastry cutter or two knives until it forms coarse, even crumbs. Stir in the walnuts. Sprinkle the crumb mixture over the apples, spooning some into the cavity of each apple and then mounding the crumb mixture over the top of the apples.

Cover the slow cooker and bake on high for 2½ to 3 hours, or until the apples are tender when pierced with a fork.

Drizzle with the maple syrup and serve warm.

TIPS:

- The grocery store is stocked with a wide range of apples, and no two are alike. Apples that soften as they cook, but generally hold their shape, are the best choice for this recipe—these include Braeburn, Rome, Granny Smith, and Golden Delicious. With any apple, for the prettiest presentation, cook until the fruit is just tender but not mushy.

- If you do not have an apple corer, use the tip of a knife to cut out the stem and the top of the apple core. Carefully, using the tip of a table knife or small spoon, scrape out the seeds and core, taking care not to cut through the bottom of the apple.

PEACH AND MANGO COBBLER

SERVES 6 TO 8 • SLOW COOKER SIZE: 3½ TO 5 QUART

What is your strongest food memory? When you think of Mom, your grandmother, or that special neighbor in the kitchen when you were a child, what food might they have been cooking? Can you almost smell it cooking, and do you long for a bite? For Kathy, that food memory is her mom baking peach cobbler, and just a whiff transports her back into the kitchen of years gone by. To this very day, a bowl of peach cobbler is a real favorite, and the addition of a mango adds a great up-to-date flavor.

Nonstick cooking spray

6 cups sliced, peeled, fresh peaches

1 medium mango, peeled, pitted, and sliced

2 tablespoons fresh lemon juice

1 cup sugar

2 tablespoons cornstarch

1 teaspoon ground cinnamon

CRUST:

1½ cups all-purpose flour

⅓ cup plus 1 tablespoon sugar

1½ teaspoons baking powder

¼ teaspoon baking soda

¼ teaspoon salt

¼ cup unsalted butter, cut into small pieces and chilled

1 cup buttermilk (see Tips, page 48)

½ teaspoon ground cinnamon

Spray a medium slow cooker with nonstick spray.

Place the peaches and mango in the slow cooker. Drizzle with the lemon juice and stir to coat evenly.

In a small bowl, stir together the sugar, cornstarch, and cinnamon. Pour the sugar mixture over the fruit in the slow cooker and stir to coat evenly. Drizzle with ⅔ cup water. Cover the slow cooker and bake on low for 2 to 2½ hours, or until the fruit is hot.

MAKE THE CRUST: In a large bowl, whisk together the flour, ⅓ cup of the sugar, the baking powder, baking soda, and salt. Cut in the butter with a pastry cutter or two knives until it forms coarse, even crumbs. Stir in the buttermilk, blending just until moistened.

Stir together the remaining 1 tablespoon sugar and the cinnamon in a small bowl.

Turn the slow cooker to high. Drop the batter by teaspoonfuls evenly across the top of the fruit. Sprinkle the cinnamon-sugar mixture evenly over the top. Cover the slow cooker and bake on high for 2 to 2½ hours, or until the edges of the crust are lightly browned and the center is dry and set.

Spoon the cobbler into individual serving dishes and serve warm.

TIPS:

- Warm cobbler topped with a scoop of vanilla ice cream is wonderful.

- Mangoes have a flat, oblong pit in the center. You will need to cut on either side of the pit, separating the flesh from the pit. Slice the fruit, trimming away the peel.

- Substitute 2 pounds frozen, sliced peaches and 1 pound frozen, cubed mango for the fresh fruits, if you wish. Pour the frozen fruit into the slow cooker and proceed as recipe directs. There is no need to thaw the fruit. Reduce the water to ⅓ cup.

BANANAS FOSTER

SERVES 4 TO 6 • SLOW COOKER SIZE: 3 TO 4 QUART

This classic recipe originated in New Orleans and still continues to be popular decades later. We like to serve this as a no-brainer dessert when entertaining. Purchase high quality ice cream to ladle the golden bananas and sauce over, and take all the credit!

½ cup unsalted butter, cut into pieces, plus more for the slow cooker

1 cup packed brown sugar

½ cup heavy cream

2 tablespoons crème de banane or dark rum

⅓ cup chopped pecans, toasted (see Tips, page 36)

¼ teaspoon ground cinnamon

3 medium bananas

Vanilla ice cream, for serving

Butter a 3- or 4-quart slow cooker.

Place the butter, brown sugar, cream, crème de banane, pecans, and cinnamon in the slow cooker. Cover the slow cooker and cook on low for 1 to 2 hours. Whisk until smooth.

Cut the bananas into ½-inch slices and add them to the slow cooker, stirring gently to coat with the brown sugar mixture. Cover the slow cooker and cook on low for 10 to 15 minutes.

Serve immediately over ice cream.

TIPS:

• **Add the banana slices just 10 to 15 minutes before serving so they do not become too soft.**

• **This is equally delicious served over pound cake or angel food cake.**

PLUM-ORANGE BROWN BETTY

SERVES 6 • SLOW COOKER SIZE: 4 QUART

Brown Betty is certainly a peculiar name! A Betty was a popular fruit dessert in the late 1800s, especially in New England. Whatever the name of this dish, who wouldn't enjoy a luscious dessert of sweetened summer-ripe plums and cinnamon-sugar-coated bread cubes? There is nothing old-fashioned about this great flavor.

Nonstick cooking spray

6 slices firm or country-style white bread (about 9 ounces), toasted

½ cup unsalted butter, melted

⅔ cup sugar

1 tablespoon ground cinnamon

FRUIT:

½ cup sugar (see Tips)

2 teaspoons cornstarch

Grated zest of 1 orange

6 medium plums, unpeeled, pitted and cut into ½-inch slices

2 tablespoons orange juice

Orange Hard Sauce (optional; recipe follows)

Line a 4-quart slow cooker with parchment paper (see page 7). Spray the parchment paper with nonstick spray.

Cut the bread into ¼- to ½-inch cubes and place them in a large bowl. Drizzle the bread cubes with the melted butter and toss to coat evenly.

Stir together the sugar and cinnamon in a small bowl. Pour the cinnamon-sugar mixture over the bread cubes and toss to coat evenly. Place the bread cubes in the slow cooker, spreading them evenly.

MAKE THE FRUIT: In a medium bowl, stir together the sugar, cornstarch, and orange zest. Stir in the sliced plums and orange juice. Spoon the fruit mixture and any collected juices evenly over the bread cubes in the slow cooker.

Cover the slow cooker and bake on low for 2½ to 3 hours, or until the fruit is tender. Unplug the slow cooker and let stand, covered, for 30 minutes.

Serve warm, spooned into individual serving bowls. Top, if desired, with a spoonful of Orange Hard Sauce.

TIPS:

- **Sweet or tart fruit? Taste a small piece of the fruit. If it tastes sweet, begin by adding ½ cup of the sugar. If the fruit is more tart, increase the sugar to ⅔ cup, or to taste.**

- **Orange zest is easy to grate using a Microplane grater. Remember that the wonderful, intense orange flavor you want is in the colored portion, but the white pith is bitter.**

ORANGE HARD SAUCE

MAKES ¾ CUP

6 tablespoons unsalted butter, at room temperature

1 cup confectioners' sugar

1 tablespoon orange juice

½ teaspoon pure vanilla extract

In a medium bowl using a hand mixer, beat the butter on medium-high speed until fluffy. Add the sugar and beat until creamy. Add the orange juice and vanilla and beat until smooth. Spoon over the Brown Betty as directed in the recipe.

TIPS:

- **What is hard sauce and when to serve it? Hard sauce is an old-fashioned sauce that classically tops plum pudding but is scrumptious on Brown Betty, bread puddings, and many other fruit desserts. The curious name refers to the fact that once made, it can be refrigerated until firm—so when a spoonful is placed on the warm dessert, the butter-rich sauce melts over the dessert. For this hard sauce, orange juice is an ideal flavoring, but rum, brandy, whiskey, liqueurs, or vanilla are a few of the flavors you can substitute for the orange juice so the hard sauce complements different desserts.**

- **If desired, spoon the prepared Orange Hard Sauce onto a sheet of plastic wrap, shaping the hard sauce roughly into a log about 1½ inches in diameter. Roll the log in the plastic wrap, covering the hard sauce completely. Refrigerate for 1 hour, or until the sauce forms a firm log. Unwrap and cut the log crosswise into slices about ¾ inch thick. Place a "disc" of the hard sauce on each serving.**

BLUEBERRY-ALMOND BUCKLE

MAKES 1 (7-INCH) CAKE • SLOW COOKER SIZE: 5 QUART OR LARGER

What is a buckle? This old-fashioned dessert features a crumb topping on a moist fruit-filled cake. The name probably came from the "buckled" irregular appearance the crumbs make on the surface of the cake. No matter what you call it, this wonderful cake would be ideal to serve as a coffee cake with breakfast or brunch or anytime friends stop by for coffee or tea.

STREUSEL:

2 tablespoons sugar

1 tablespoon all-purpose flour

2 tablespoons unsalted butter, cut into small pieces and chilled

⅓ cup sliced almonds, toasted

CAKE:

Butter and all-purpose flour, for the pan

1 cup fresh blueberries

1 cup plus 2 tablespoons all-purpose flour

1½ teaspoons baking powder

Dash of salt

¼ cup unsalted butter, at room temperature

⅓ cup sugar

1 large egg, at room temperature

⅓ cup whole milk

½ teaspoon pure vanilla extract

¼ teaspoon pure almond extract

Butter and flour a 7-inch springform pan. Crumple a sheet of aluminum foil, about 24 inches long, into a thin strip, then form it into a 7-inch ring. Place the ring in the bottom of a large slow cooker.

MAKE THE STREUSEL: In a small bowl, stir together the sugar and flour. Cut in the butter with a pastry cutter or two knives until the mixture forms coarse, even crumbs. Stir in the almonds and set aside.

MAKE THE CAKE: In a small bowl, toss the blueberries with 2 tablespoons of the flour; set aside.

In a small bowl, whisk together the remaining 1 cup flour, the baking powder, and the salt; set aside.

In a large bowl using a hand mixer, beat together the butter and sugar on medium-high speed until light and fluffy. Beat in the egg.

Add the flour mixture alternately with the milk to the butter mixture, making three additions of the flour and two of the milk. Beat in the vanilla and almond extract.

Stir the blueberries into the batter.

Spoon the batter into the prepared pan. Sprinkle the streusel mixture evenly over the top of the batter.

Place the filled springform pan on the foil ring in the slow cooker. Cover the slow cooker and bake on high for 2½ to 3 hours, or until a wooden pick inserted into the center of the cake comes out clean.

Transfer the pan to a wire rack to cool for 10 minutes. Remove the outer ring from the pan and let the cake cool completely. Serve warm.

TIPS:

- **Toasting almonds intensifies their flavor. To toast almonds, spread them in a single layer on a rimmed baking sheet. Bake at 350°F for 5 to 7 minutes, or until lightly toasted.**

- **This is wonderful when fresh blueberries are in season. If fresh are not available, substitute frozen. Toss the frozen blueberries in the flour and proceed as directed in the recipe.**

WINE-POACHED PEARS WITH BUTTERSCOTCH SAUCE

SERVES 6 • SLOW COOKER SIZE: 5 QUART OR LARGER

Divine elegance. There is just no other way to describe this perfect dish. It is beautiful, and the warm pears coated in the luscious sauce taste fantastic.

Nonstick cooking spray

6 medium pears, preferably Bosc

2 tablespoons fresh lemon juice

½ cup sugar

¾ cup dry white wine, such as Chardonnay

1 teaspoon pure vanilla extract

BUTTERSCOTCH SAUCE:

6 tablespoons unsalted butter

¾ cup packed brown sugar

Dash of salt

½ cup heavy cream

2 teaspoons pure vanilla extract

Spray a large slow cooker with nonstick spray.

Peel the pears, leaving the stem intact. Stand the pears upright in the slow cooker. Brush the pears with the lemon juice. Sprinkle the pears with the sugar. Pour in the wine, vanilla, and 3 cups water.

Cover the slow cooker and cook on low for 3½ to 4 hours, or until the pears are tender when pricked with a fork but not mushy.

MAKE THE BUTTERSCOTCH SAUCE: Melt the butter in a small saucepan over medium heat. Stir in the brown sugar and salt and cook, stirring continuously, for 1 minute, or until bubbling. Stir in the cream and cook, stirring continuously, for 2 to 3 minutes, or until bubbling. Stir in the vanilla. Let stand for 5 to 10 minutes to thicken.

Use a slotted spoon to lift the pears out of the poaching liquid and place each on an individual serving plate. Drizzle the pears with the butterscotch sauce. Serve warm.

TIPS:

- **Pears range from golden to green to red. Many varieties are great to eat fresh or sliced in salads or for appetizers, while others are ideal for baking. The earthy light brown, cinnamon-colored Bosc pear, known for its long, tapered neck, is recommended for this recipe as it holds its shape when baked, so once topped with the warm butterscotch sauce, the finished dish will be beautiful.**

CINNAMON-CALVADOS APPLESAUCE

MAKES 4 CUPS • SLOW COOKER SIZE: 4 QUART

Yes, grown-ups will now enjoy this up-to-date version of an old-fashioned classic. When you discover how simple this spice-studded side dish or dessert is to prepare, it will become a staple in your recipe box.

Nonstick cooking spray

8 medium Granny Smith apples, peeled, cored, and sliced

⅔ cup sugar

½ cup apple juice or apple cider

½ cup Calvados

2 tablespoons unsalted butter, cut into small cubes

1 teaspoon ground cinnamon

¼ teaspoon ground nutmeg

Spray a 4-quart slow cooker with nonstick spray.

Place all the ingredients in the slow cooker and stir to combine.

Cover the slow cooker and cook on high for 2½ to 3 hours, or until the apple pieces begin to break down. Stir until the applesauce reaches the desired consistency (smooth or slightly chunky).

Serve warm or chilled.

TIPS:

- If desired, omit the brandy and increase the apple juice to 1 cup.

- Calvados is a famous French apple brandy, and it adds an unbeatable flavor to this applesauce. Yes, apple brandy from the United States, such as applejack, can be substituted for the Calvados.

- Apple varieties seem to have exploded in recent years, and grocery stores stock an entire aisle of apples. We like to use Granny Smith apples in this recipe, but some of our other favorite varieties for applesauce include Jonathan, Golden Delicious, Jonagold, McIntosh, and Braeburn. Each region also has favorite varieties, and we often combine several types of apple in one batch of applesauce.

CHERRY CLAFOUTIS

SERVES 6 TO 8 · SLOW COOKER SIZE: 4 TO 5 QUART

When a ticket to the south of France is out of the question, why not indulge and enjoy this cherry clafoutis? A clafoutis is a baked French dessert of fruit, usually cherries, arranged in a buttered dish and covered with a pancake-type batter. It is best baked and served warm, sprinkled with confectioners' sugar. The slow cooker provides an excellent method for baking a moist yet flavorful clafoutis.

1 (12-ounce) bag frozen unsweetened dark sweet cherries

3 ounces cream cheese, at room temperature

2 large eggs, at room temperature

½ cup sugar

⅓ cup all-purpose flour

½ cup whole milk

Pinch of salt

½ teaspoon pure vanilla extract

1 tablespoon unsalted butter, melted, plus more for the slow cooker

Confectioners' sugar, for dusting

Generously butter the bottom and 2 inches up the sides of a 4- or 5-quart slow cooker.

Place the cherries evenly over the bottom of the slow cooker.

In a blender, combine the cream cheese, eggs, sugar, flour, milk, salt, vanilla, and melted butter and blend until smooth. Pour the batter over the cherries in the slow cooker.

Cover the slow cooker and bake on high for 1½ to 2½ hours, or until the center of the clafoutis is just set. Unplug the slow cooker and let stand, covered, for 30 minutes.

Dust the clafoutis generously with confectioners' sugar. Serve warm.

TIP:

• **If you find your slow cooker is a little hotter and the sides of delicate dishes, such as this clafoutis, brown too quickly, you can line the slow cooker with parchment paper—see page 7 for instructions.**

APPLE BUTTER

MAKES ABOUT 4 CUPS · SLOW COOKER SIZE: 5 QUART OR LARGER

We like to make this fruit butter to give as a gift with muffins, fruit breads, and scones.

Nonstick cooking spray

10 medium apples, preferably a combination of Granny Smith and Jonathan

1⅓ cups packed brown sugar

¾ cup apple juice or apple cider

1 tablespoon ground cinnamon

Juice of 1 lemon

1 teaspoon ground allspice

1 teaspoon ground nutmeg

½ teaspoon ground cloves

Spray a large slow cooker with nonstick spray.

Core and quarter the apples, but do not peel them. Combine the apples and the remaining ingredients in the slow cooker. Cover the slow cooker and cook on low for 8 to 10 hours.

Mash the apples directly in the slow cooker with a potato masher or large fork.

Cook, uncovered, on high for 2 hours, or until thick.

Spoon the apple butter into a refrigerator container and store, covered, in the refrigerator for up to 6 months.

TIPS:

- **Making a thick and flavorful fruit butter takes a long time. This is a great recipe to cook overnight, so it simmers and thickens while you sleep. As an added bonus, you can spread the warm, freshly prepared apple butter on your toast for breakfast. Oh my, it is good.**

- **Store the apple butter in the refrigerator since it has not been canned according to recommended USDA processing methods.**

INSIDE-OUT CARAMEL APPLES

SERVES 6 • SLOW COOKER SIZE: 5 QUART OR LARGER

There is something special about a crisp fall day, a stroll through the local community fair or festival, and a bite of a caramel apple. They just go together, and the combination is irresistible. This easy, fun version of that classic does not require sticks, outdoor fairs, or even waiting until fall. Just three ingredients and a slow cooker are all that is needed.

Nonstick cooking spray

6 medium apples, unpeeled (see Tips)

1 cup caramel bits (see Tips)

5 tablespoons heavy cream

Spray a large slow cooker with nonstick spray.

Use an apple corer to core the apple, carefully scraping out the seeds and core, but taking care not to cut through the bottom of the apple.

Set the apples upright in the slow cooker. Spoon a scant tablespoon of caramel bits into the cavity of each apple; set aside the remaining caramel bits. Drizzle 1½ teaspoons of the cream into each apple cavity, reserving the remaining cream.

Cover the slow cooker and bake on low for 2½ to 3½ hours, until the apples are tender when pricked with the tip of a knife. Using a large, slotted spoon, carefully lift out each apple and place it in an individual serving dish.

Combine the remaining caramel bits and cream in a microwave-safe 2-cup glass bowl and microwave on high (100 percent) power for 30 seconds. Stir and continue to microwave for 30 to 40 seconds, or until the mixture is hot and bubbling. Stir until the caramel sauce is smooth.

Drizzle the warm caramel sauce over the apples. Serve warm.

TIPS:

- Select firm apples, such as Rome, Braeburn, or Granny Smith. These apples cook nicely, yet hold their shape.

- If desired, serve warm apples topped with a scoop of cinnamon or butter brickle ice cream or a dollop of whipped cream.

- Caramel bits are small pieces of chewy caramel candies, each about ⅜ inch in diameter and unwrapped. They are ideal to use for this recipe. If caramel bits are not available, substitute caramels—unwrap and cut them into about ⅜-inch pieces. Approximately 24 caramels chopped will equal about 1 cup caramel bits.

PEACH BUTTER

MAKES 4 CUPS • SLOW COOKER SIZE: 5 QUART OR LARGER

Capture the flavor of summer's best peaches with this fruit butter recipe. We gave the classic flavor just a little twist thanks to the orange juice and ginger.

Nonstick cooking spray

12 medium peaches, pitted, peeled, and sliced

3 tablespoons orange juice

1 tablespoon fresh lemon juice

2¾ cups sugar

¼ to ½ teaspoon ground ginger

Spray a large slow cooker with nonstick spray.

Place the peaches in the slow cooker and add the orange juice and lemon juice. Stir to coat evenly.

Cover the slow cooker and cook on low for 3 to 3½ hours, or until the peaches are very tender. Unplug the slow cooker and let the peaches cool slightly. Carefully puree the fruit directly in the slow cooker using an immersion blender. Alternatively, working in batches, ladle the fruit into a blender, blend until smooth, and return the puree to the slow cooker. (You should have about 6 cups of peach puree.)

Stir in the sugar and ginger. Cover the slow cooker and cook on high for 1 hour, or until puree is boiling. Uncover and cook on high for 5 to 6 hours, or until the peach butter is as thick as desired.

Spoon the peach butter into a refrigerator container and store, covered, in the refrigerator for up to 6 months.

TIPS:

• The sweetness of the ripe peaches varies, so it is wise to carefully taste a small amount of the peach butter partway through the cooking process and add additional sugar to taste, if desired.

• Using an immersion blender or a typical countertop blender makes a peach butter that is smooth. If you prefer a more chunky texture, use a potato masher to mash the cooked peaches directly in the slow cooker.

• Use caution when blending the hot fruit. If using a countertop blender, vent the cover to allow the steam to escape.

• Store the peach butter in the refrigerator since it has not been canned according to recommended USDA processing methods.

BRANDIED PEACH JUBILEE

SERVES 6 • SLOW COOKER SIZE: 3½ TO 5 QUART

While cherries jubilee is a classic dish, we think it just might pale in comparison to this Brandied Peach Jubilee. Spoon the warm peaches over dishes of ice cream, bowls of frozen yogurt, or slices of pound cake. Wow!

Nonstick cooking spray

4 cups sliced, peeled, fresh peaches

2 tablespoons fresh lemon juice

¾ cup sugar

3 tablespoons cornstarch

2 tablespoons unsalted butter, cut into small pieces

2 tablespoons brandy

Ice cream, frozen yogurt, or pound cake slices, for serving

Spray a medium slow cooker with nonstick spray.

Place the peaches in the slow cooker and toss with the lemon juice.

Stir together the sugar and cornstarch in a small bowl. Pour the sugar mixture over the peaches and stir to coat evenly. Dot with the butter.

Cover the slow cooker and cook on low for 2½ to 3 hours, or until the peaches are tender and the juices are thickened and bubbling.

Stir in the brandy. Serve warm, over ice cream.

TIP:

- **If desired, substitute 2 pounds frozen peaches. No need to thaw them—just use them as directed in the recipe.**

CANDIED CRANBERRY AND CRYSTALLIZED GINGER CHUTNEY

MAKES ABOUT 3 CUPS • SLOW COOKER SIZE: 3½ TO 5 QUART

When do you serve a flavorful chutney? Sure, you can serve it as a tasty accompaniment to roasted turkey at Thanksgiving or with roast pork anytime, and it is fantastic with grilled chicken or pork, but once you make this chutney, you will be dreaming of all kinds of appetizers and desserts. See the tips for some inspiration.

Nonstick cooking spray

4 cups fresh cranberries, or 1 (16-ounce) package frozen cranberries

1¼ cups sugar

1 (2.7-ounce) jar crystallized ginger, chopped (about ⅓ cup)

½ cup dried apricots, finely chopped

½ teaspoon ground cinnamon

Dash of salt

2 tablespoons orange juice

1 tablespoon raspberry vinegar or red wine vinegar

1 to 2 tablespoons orange-, cranberry-, or ginger-flavored liqueur (optional)

Spray a medium slow cooker with nonstick spray.

Combine the cranberries, sugar, ginger, apricots, cinnamon, salt, orange juice, and vinegar in the slow cooker. Cover the slow cooker and cook on low for 5 to 7 hours, or until the fruit is tender and the mixture is bubbling. (It will be thin.)

Unplug and uncover the slow cooker. Let the chutney cool for 1 hour. Ladle the chutney into a refrigerator container. Cover and refrigerate for several hours or overnight, until the chutney is chilled and thick. If desired, stir in the liqueur.

Store the chutney, covered, in the refrigerator for up to 6 months.

TIPS:

- Do you enjoy sweeter flavors? Carefully spoon out a little, let it cool, and taste the hot cranberry mixture during the last 1 to 2 hours of cooking. If you prefer a sweeter flavor, stir in 2 to 3 tablespoons sugar, or to taste. Cover the slow cooker and continue cooking.

- The chutney will be thin, more like the consistency of syrup, when hot. Do not be concerned—it will thicken as it chills in the refrigerator.

- Store the chutney in the refrigerator since it has not been canned according to recommended USDA processing methods.

- When to serve this chutney? Spoon some onto cream cheese and serve as a spread on crackers. Or dollop some on top of a wheel of Brie, add to a grilled cheese sandwich, spread on warm scones, or accompany a slice of pound cake. For a special dessert, lightly toast or grill pound cake slices, then dollop with chutney and whipped cream.

FONDUES
and
CONFECTIONS

CHOCOLATE CASHEW CLUSTERS

MAKES ABOUT 6½ DOZEN CANDIES • SLOW COOKER SIZE: 3½ TO 5 QUART

Candymaking time will never feel intimidating again. Just fill the slow cooker and let it do its magic for an hour and a half. Dip out those favorite Chocolate Cashew Clusters, and you will be known far and wide as a candymaker extraordinaire!

Nonstick cooking spray

1 (14-ounce) can salted cashew halves

2 (12-ounce) packages semisweet chocolate chips

1 (12-ounce) package milk chocolate chips

1 (3.5-ounce) dark chocolate candy bar, broken into pieces

4 ounces chocolate-flavored candy coating, chopped into 1- to 2-inch pieces (see Tip)

Spray a medium slow cooker with nonstick spray. Line a baking sheet with parchment paper or waxed paper.

Place the ingredients in the slow cooker in the order listed. Do not stir. Cover the slow cooker and cook on low for 1½ hours. Stir until combined. If the chocolate is not fully melted, cover and cook on low for 15 to 30 minutes more, or until melted. Stir until well combined.

Drop the candies by tablespoonful onto the lined baking sheet. Let cool until set, 3 to 5 hours.

Store the candies in airtight containers at room temperature for up to 1 week.

TIP:

• **The chocolate-flavored candy coating may be known as almond bark. It is readily available at most grocery stores in the baking aisle. Break off the amount you need, then seal any remaining in a zip-top plastic bag or wrap tightly in plastic wrap and use within 2 years.**

CRISPY PEANUT BUTTER CANDY

MAKES ABOUT 8 DOZEN CANDIES • SLOW COOKER SIZE: 5 QUART OR LARGER

Roxanne's daughter, Grace, was lucky enough to have a terrific piano teacher who understood how to inspire her students. An added benefit of practicing was the treats Sherri Wolverton would share. This is an adaptation of a recipe that Sherri served as treats to entice her students to do their best work. Thanks, Sherri.

Nonstick cooking spray

2 (24-ounce) packages vanilla-flavored candy coating (see Tips)

3 cups creamy peanut butter

1 (9-ounce) box toasted rice cereal, such as Rice Krispies

1 (10-ounce) bag miniature marshmallows

2 cups candy-coated chocolate pieces, such as M&M's

Spray an 18 x 12–inch baking sheet with nonstick spray. Spray a large slow cooker with nonstick spray.

Chop the candy coating into 1- to 2-inch pieces. Place them in the slow cooker. Cover the slow cooker and cook on low for 45 minutes to 1 hour, stirring occasionally, until the candy is melted.

Unplug the slow cooker and add the peanut butter. Stir until the mixture is smooth. Add the cereal and stir to blend well. Fold in the marshmallows and 1½ cups of the chocolate pieces.

Spread the mixture evenly over the prepared pan and press with a spatula to compact the mixture. Sprinkle evenly with the remaining ½ cup chocolate pieces.

Let set and cool completely, then cut into squares.

- Refrigerate to accelerate the setting process.

- Use a cookie cutter and cut the candy into fun shapes, or use a knife to cut it into diamond shapes.

- The vanilla-flavored candy coating may be known as almond bark. It is readily available at most grocery stores in the baking aisle. Break off the amount you need, then seal any remaining in a zip-top plastic bag or wrap tightly in plastic wrap and use within 2 years.

FLEUR DE SEL CARAMEL FONDUE

MAKES 3 CUPS • SLOW COOKER SIZE: 1 TO 2 QUART

Sweet and salty is a captivating flavor combo, and the hint of salt in this caramel fondue boosts the flavor from great to over the moon.

Nonstick cooking spray

1 (14-ounce) package caramels, unwrapped

4½ cups miniature marshmallows (about half a 16-ounce package)

½ cup heavy cream

1½ teaspoons *fleur de sel* (see Tips)

SUGGESTIONS FOR SERVING:

Apple wedges, pear wedges, strawberries, brownie bites, pound cake cubes, bananas, or pretzels

Spray a small slow cooker with nonstick spray.

Place the caramels, marshmallows, and cream in the slow cooker. Cover the slow cooker and cook on low for 2 hours, or until melted, stirring every 30 minutes. Stir in the *fleur de sel*.

Serve warm.

TIPS:

• If desired, add an additional ½ teaspoon *fleur de sel*, or to taste.

• *Fleur de sel* is a delicately flavored sea salt, so it is typically added to the food just before serving. Due to its cost, it is often thought of as a special-occasion salt. If desired, you may substitute another sea salt in this fondue.

• Cut apples, pears, or bananas for dipping just before serving. To prevent the cut fruit from darkening, quickly toss it in lemon juice, then drain and serve.

• Serving fondue in a slow cooker is a perfect way to keep it warm. Some small slow cookers have a warm setting, which is ideal to use. For other slow cookers, use the low setting and stir the fondue occasionally. For a dinner party, you might find you prefer to prepare the fondue in the slow cooker in the kitchen, then transfer it to a fondue pot for serving. Be sure to set out plenty of fondue forks.

ELEGANT CHOCOLATE FONDUE

MAKES ABOUT 3 CUPS • SLOW COOKER SIZE: 1 TO 2 QUART

Fuss-free entertaining equates to fondue. The "wow" factor is not only the creamy, decadent, smooth fondue sauce but also the way that you arrange the suggested dippers on a large platter. Have fun and use this recipe as an excuse to celebrate a great report card, an anniversary, or even a surprise snow day!

Nonstick cooking spray

1 (9.3-ounce) package milk chocolate candy bars (6 candy bars)

1 (4-ounce) bar bittersweet chocolate

1 tablespoon unsalted butter

25 large marshmallows

1¼ cups heavy cream

SUGGESTIONS FOR SERVING:

Strawberries, bananas, brownie bites, pound cake cubes, marshmallows, pretzels, or maraschino cherries

Spray a small slow cooker with nonstick spray.

Break the milk chocolate and bittersweet chocolate into small pieces and place in the slow cooker. Add the remaining ingredients and stir to combine.

Cover the slow cooker and cook on low for 1 hour, or until melted, stirring every 30 minutes. Stir until combined.

Serve warm.

TIP:

- **You can substitute semisweet or other varieties of chocolate for either the milk or bittersweet chocolate. Any chocolate flavor that you prefer would work well.**

BUTTERSCOTCH FONDUE

MAKES 4 CUPS • SLOW COOKER SIZE: 1 TO 2 QUART

Warm butterscotch, that incredible butter and brown sugar sauce, is a timeless fondue that tastes fantastic. It is a versatile flavor—you can serve the fondue with pieces of fruit, cake, cookies, or pretzels, or for a change, ladle the warm fondue over your favorite ice cream or dessert.

Nonstick cooking spray

½ cup unsalted butter, cut into pieces

1½ cups packed brown sugar

1 (14-ounce) can sweetened condensed milk

1 cup heavy cream

1 teaspoon pure vanilla extract

SUGGESTIONS FOR SERVING:

Bananas, apple wedges, pear wedges, brownie bites, pound cake cubes, graham crackers, sugar cookies, pecan shortbread cookies, or pretzel sticks

Spray a small slow cooker with nonstick spray.

Combine the butter, brown sugar, and condensed milk in the slow cooker. Cover the slow cooker and cook on high for 1 to 1½ hours, or until the mixture is hot and bubbling and the sugar has dissolved, stirring every 30 minutes.

Stir in the cream and vanilla. Cover the slow cooker and cook on low for 15 minutes more. Stir until blended.

Serve warm.

TIPS:

- **Fondues are created for dipping, but all of the fondues in this cookbook are great if ladled warm over bowls of ice cream or cake. We also like to grill pineapple wedges, or peach or nectarine halves, just until warm and grill marks are evident, place them in individual dessert bowls, and then spoon the warm fondue over them.**

- **Cut apples, pears, or bananas for dipping just before serving. To prevent the cut fruit from darkening, quickly toss it in lemon juice, then drain and serve.**

WHITE CHOCOLATE FONDUE

MAKES ABOUT 2½ CUPS • SLOW COOKER SIZE: 1 TO 2 QUART

This creamy, sweet fondue is elegant, so it is the ideal dessert to serve at your next party. The great flavor and beautiful appearance will make it a hit.

Nonstick cooking spray

4 (4-ounce) packages white chocolate

1 cup heavy cream

SUGGESTIONS FOR SERVING:

Strawberries, firm raspberries or blackberries, brownie bites, pound cake cubes, or maraschino cherries

Spray a small slow cooker with nonstick spray.

Break the white chocolate into small pieces and place them in the slow cooker. Drizzle with ½ cup of the cream.

Cover the slow cooker and cook on low for 1 hour, or until melted and smooth, stirring every 30 minutes. Stir until combined.

Stir in the remaining cream, blending until smooth.

Serve warm.

TIPS:

- **Stir in 2 tablespoons Frangelico, amaretto, white chocolate liqueur, or Grand Marnier just before serving, if desired.**

- **Choose a good quality white chocolate, one that lists cocoa butter in the ingredient list, for the best flavor in this fondue recipe.**

CANDY BAR FONDUE

MAKES 3 CUPS · SLOW COOKER SIZE: 1 TO 2 QUART

This incredible fondue tastes like delicious warm candy and flows like sweet lava over cookies, cake, or other foods.

Nonstick cooking spray

1 (12-ounce) package milk chocolate chips

1 (7-ounce) jar marshmallow creme

25 caramels, unwrapped

½ cup heavy cream

1 (3.36-ounce) package fun-size caramel, chocolate, and nougat candy bars, such as Milky Way, chopped (6 small candy bars)

SUGGESTIONS FOR SERVING:

Chocolate or vanilla cookies, pretzel sticks, brownie bites, pound cake cubes, or graham crackers

Spray a small slow cooker with nonstick spray.

Place all the ingredients in the slow cooker. Cover the slow cooker and cook on low for 1½ to 2 hours, or until melted and smooth, stirring every 30 minutes. Stir until combined.

Serve warm.

TIPS:

- **Candy bars come in all sizes. Substitute ¾ cup chopped candy bars for the fun-size package listed in the recipe. For a change, substitute an equal amount of other creamy chocolate and caramel candy bars.**

- **Leftover fondue? Spoon into refrigerator containers, cover, and refrigerate for up to 1 week. When ready to serve, spoon into a microwave-safe glass bowl and microwave just until the fondue is warm. Stir well, then spoon over bowls of ice cream, frozen yogurt, or cake.**

FRENCH QUARTER PRALINE DIP

MAKES 3 CUPS • SLOW COOKER SIZE: 1 TO 2 QUART

Magnolia blossoms, fried green tomatoes, fried chicken, boiled peanuts, and pralines remind Roxanne of her beloved South. She likes to claim being born in Missouri as enough ties to the South, but given any excuse to move to the Carolinas, Georgia, Louisiana, or Tennessee, she will be gone in a heartbeat. In the meantime, she enjoys this dip and serves it to her husband so they can dream once again of living in the South.

Nonstick cooking spray

1 cup packed brown sugar

¼ cup sugar

½ teaspoon ground cinnamon

¼ cup dark corn syrup

¼ cup light corn syrup

⅓ cup chopped pecans, toasted (see Tips, page 36)

1¼ cups heavy cream

½ teaspoon pure vanilla extract

SUGGESTIONS FOR SERVING:

Pound cake cubes, bananas, shortbread cookies, doughnut holes, beignets

Spray a small slow cooker with nonstick spray.

Combine all the ingredients, except the vanilla, in the slow cooker. Cover the slow cooker and cook on high for 1½ to 2½ hours, or until a thermometer inserted into the mixture reads 220°F.

Stir in the vanilla. Whisk until smooth. Unplug the slow cooker and let stand, covered, for 1 hour. Stir before serving.

Serve warm.

TIPS:

- Warm French Quarter Praline Dip makes an irresistible dessert sauce. Ladle the wonderful sauce over Praline-Pecan Bread Pudding (page 66) or over bowls of ice cream, cake, bread pudding, or cobbler.

- Cut bananas for dipping just before serving. To prevent the bananas from darkening, quickly toss them in lemon juice, then drain and serve.

FONDUE FAVORITES

Fondue is especially fun and tasty if you offer a variety of foods for dipping. Be creative! Cut the food into bite-size cubes, wedges, or pieces. Be sure to set out plenty of fondue forks. Some of our favorites include:

Cake, such as:
- Angel food cake
- Pound cake (any flavor)

Cake pops

Cookies and brownies, such as:
- Brownies
- Chocolate wafers
- Cream-filled sandwich cookies
- Gingersnaps
- Pirouette cookies
- Shortbread cookies
- Sugar cookies

Snacks:
- Graham crackers
- Pretzels

Sweet Rolls:
- Beignets
- Cinnamon rolls
- Doughnut holes

Fruit

FRESH:
- Apples
- Bananas
- Blackberries or raspberries (firm)
- Cherries (pitted)
- Grapefruit segments
- Mandarin oranges
- Orange segments
- Pears
- Pineapple
- Strawberries

DRIED:
- Apples
- Apricots
- Mangoes
- Pineapple

JARRED:
- Maraschino cherries

ACKNOWLEDGMENTS

This collection of recipes brings us full circle, for we started our careers working with slow cookers. Now, years later, we cherish the path that has brought us to this point and are grateful for the many people who have supported us on this journey.

Our families mean everything to us.

Roxanne's family: To my husband, Bob Bateman, thank you for living the sweet dream with me for more than twenty-two years! Your support, encouragement, and love have been my inspiration. To my daughter, Grace, thank you for your pure love and sweetness. You have tasted, tested, and taken food field trips your entire life and enjoyed the adventure. Thank you for filling our world with joy. I am grateful to my mom and dad for the depth of their love and for teaching me the love and joy of a family. To my mom, Colleen Wyss, thank you for your love of baking and for showing me the joy of spending time in the kitchen. You have been our biggest cheerleader for slow cooker cakes and cheesecakes—thank you! And last, but certainly not least, basketfuls of thanks to Kathy. You have added so much sugar and spice to my life for more than thirty years. Your attention to the details of running a business has allowed me the freedom to dream bigger dreams for us. Here's to many more years of baking and enjoying the sweet life!

Kathy's family: To my husband, David, and daughters, Laura and Amanda, who fill my life with love and joy. Throughout it all—from countless groceries and dirty dishes to late nights at the computer—your love and support make each day sweeter. Your smiles are the center of my world and I love and cherish each one of you. Each cookbook is packed with love and gratitude to my parents, who taught me to love and to follow my dreams. Thank you, Roxanne, for dreaming big dreams and for always sprinkling our work with so much laughter.

We are grateful for our absolutely fantastic agents. Lisa Ekus, Sally Ekus, and the entire staff at the Lisa Ekus Group, LLC, are wonderful, and we so appreciate their advice, wise counsel, and friendship.

We are grateful to BJ Berti and everyone at St. Martin's Press for guiding us and creating such a magnificent book. Thank you for being a wonderful team and sharing the vision for this book with us.

We are indebted to Jennifer Davick for making the recipes in this book come alive so beautifully. Jennifer and the food stylist James Herrin created a mouthwatering book, and we so appreciate their extraordinary skill and dedication.

We met in a test kitchen cooking side by side, and now, some thirty years later, we appreciate the skills we sharpened and the friendship we created. Our background has led us to wonderful places, memorable moments, and incredible opportunities, and better yet, our friendship has blessed us and made the journey so much more fun and rewarding.

We are grateful for the many wonderful people who have supported us! We appreciate each of you and want to thank you.

INDEX

ABOUT THE AUTHORS

Roxanne Wyss and **Kathy Moore** are cookbook authors, food consultants, cooking teachers, and food bloggers who share their test-kitchen expertise through creative recipes and tips that make cooking easier and more fun. Together they've written seven cookbooks, including *The Newlywed Cookbook: Cooking Happily Ever After*. They also frequently teach cooking classes and consult with food and appliance companies. Their professional careers in food span almost thirty years and now include a popular blog, www.pluggedintocooking.com.